ENGLISH
CATHEDRALS

By the same author

Charles Dickens's London

ENGLISH CATHEDRALS

ANDREW SANDERS

ROBERT HALE • LONDON

© Andrew Sanders 2015
First published in Great Britain 2015

ISBN 978-0-7198-1659-8

Robert Hale Limited
Clerkenwell House
Clerkenwell Green
London EC1R 0HT

www.halebooks.com

A catalogue record for this book is available from the British Library

2 4 6 8 10 9 7 5 3 1

Printed in Czech Republic

CONTENTS

INTRODUCTION

SOME YEARS AGO, WHEN Palace Green, the expansive lawn on the north flank of Durham Cathedral, was thronged with students, their families and the academic community during one of the University of Durham's summer graduation ceremonies, an American tourist, who had somehow got mixed up in the throng, asked me, 'Where is the cathedral?' At the time it seemed like an absurd question. Of all the English cathedrals, Durham's is perhaps the least mistakeably a cathedral. It really could not be anything other than a cathedral. And the great church was facing the American head-on. Admittedly, Palace Green is surrounded by many venerable stone buildings, most of which now are attached to the university, but the cathedral does more than hold its own: it completely dominates the space just as it dominates the city of Durham. On reflection, however, this tourist's seemingly naïve question had some foundation. Many American universities actually look like cathedrals (as any visitor to Durham, North Carolina, would readily acknowledge). It was clear that my questioner had not brought a good guidebook with her and she certainly had not read the acclaim accorded to Durham Cathedral by two earlier American visitors. In the 1840s, the writer Nathaniel Hawthorne had insisted that he had never seen 'so lovely and magnificent a scene' and some one hundred and fifty years later, another writer, Bill Bryson, had extravagantly proclaimed that Durham was 'the best cathedral on planet earth'. Nevertheless, my so-far unimpressed questioner still needed to discover the extraordinary individuality of Durham Cathedral for herself and, moreover, to grasp what distinguishes this and all other cathedrals from secular buildings, however 'awesome' they may seem at first sight.

We use the term 'cathedral' very loosely nowadays. Large parish churches are sometimes dignified with the epithet 'the cathedral of the Broads' or 'the cathedral of the Wolds' when they are nothing of the kind. There are caves, forest-clearings and avenues of trees that are described as being like 'cathedrals'. In common parlance, too, there are 'cathedrals of learning' (like Duke University at Durham, North Carolina); there are 'cathedrals of industry' (any number of power stations or great factory buildings might qualify) and 'cathedrals of commerce' (one only has to think of distant views of Manhattan or Chicago, or even of Canary Wharf). A recent commentator has gone so far as to describe Selfridges department store in London as a prime example of a 'cathedral of commerce' (perhaps because the alternative cognomen 'cathedral of consumerism' eluded him). All of these buildings can be said to inspire a variety of 'awesome' experiences, whether they be new experiences of space, or height, or an overwhelming sense of visual and tactile satisfaction. The twentieth century produced only a sprinkling of great churches, but certain of its architects proved themselves adept at inspiring awe when they were empowered to create educational, industrial and commercial spaces that were both grand and beautiful. But a building that may strike over-imaginative commentators as a 'cathedral' does not actually render it a cathedral, either in form or in purpose.

A 'cathedral' has always had, and still has, a very specific function. That function is more clearly defined than that of a Neo-Gothic university campus or of a soaring atrium in an Art-Deco commercial block or even of a cleanly functional Modern Movement factory. Indeed, universities, office blocks and factories have multiple functions. A cathedral has only one. A cathedral is a bishop's church, dedicated to the worship of God and designed to contain dignified Christian worship (and especially *choral* worship). A cathedral is not a sanctified aircraft hangar, however much it might look like one. Without a bishop and, more significantly, without a semblance of the religious rituals for which it was built, a cathedral loses its proper purpose and its soul. Only then does it resemble a hangar, though no aircraft or airship could be squeezed through its narrow portals. Great churches are not particularly versatile spaces unless they remain dedicated to religious uses. They make embarrassingly soulless museums (as anyone who remembers the deconsecrated cathedrals of Soviet Russia will know). Historically, reuse or inappropriate adaptation has entailed architectural and structural distortion. Redundancy has gone hand in hand with desecration. The Gothic cathedrals of Nicosia and Famagusta were awkwardly re-orientated as whitewashed mosques by the Turkish conquerors of Cyprus. Scottish Presbyterians abandoned the great cathedrals of St Andrews and Elgin to ruin, and they once crudely transformed that of Glasgow into two preaching houses to house two distinct congregations (a similar fate briefly befell Exeter Cathedral during the Commonwealth, but that crime was undone in 1660). Urban churches – and cathedrals were almost by definition urban – fared better than rural abbeys. Once the monastic communities were dissolved, the remoter medieval abbey churches of Europe were stripped of their fittings and then either demolished or left desolate, whether by Henry VIII's commissioners in England or by Lutheran princes in Germany or by the anti-clerical Revolutionary government in France. Cluny in Burgundy, and the abbeys of St Martin at Tours and of St Edmund at St Edmundsbury are now no more than fragmentary ruins, while the Cistercian abbeys at Fountains in Yorkshire and Chorin in Brandenburg are now melancholy, if superbly romantic, ruins.

Blessedly, no English cathedral church suffered the fate of the Scottish cathedrals at the time of the Reformation. England retained its bishops. Scotland did not. The loss of the substantial Romanesque cathedral of St Mary at Coventry is an exception to the rule, but that church was effectively subsidiary to the then Bishop of Lichfield and Coventry's main cathedral at Lichfield (St Mary's was a monastic foundation, whereas the cathedral at Lichfield was a secular foundation). The other major loss of an English medieval cathedral was the result of a natural disaster rather than the consequence of politics or economics. St Paul's in London was burned to a shell during the Great Fire of 1666, but it was triumphantly replaced by one of the greatest of seventeenth-century churches. The new St Paul's may not have looked like its predecessor, but it is in every sense emphatically a cathedral. It is distinctively Anglican in terms of its constitution and worship, but it is also a reaffirmation of the place of the Church of England in the mainstream of Christian culture in Europe.

As we will see later in this study, Anglican cathedral establishments were indeed *distinctive* by the time St Paul's was rebuilt. Not only had the ancient Catholic sees of England been retained as essential to the new post-Reformation Anglican Settlement, so too were the bishops, their titles and their cathedrals. Indeed, Henry VIII added six new bishoprics, all of which were established in historic, formerly monastic, churches. What made the new Anglican order different from its European counterparts was that the cathedral clergy were now married. The Lutheran churches of Germany and Scandinavia had, for the most part, abolished both their bishops and the cathedral chapters that were integral to the administration of, and the worship in, bishop's churches. In Catholic lands, where prelates and cathedral chapters remained relatively untouched by the Reformation, priests remained celibate. What emerged in England was unique: a cathedral close that was no longer the exclusive preserve of men (though women were still excluded from Holy Orders). Following the Tudor Reformation of the Church of England, the nature of each cathedral chapter had been subject to a radical re-ordering (including a substantial reduction of their financial resources), and the old monastic cathedrals lost the monks that had served them for centuries. Despite this, the English cathedrals continued to offer a regular pattern of liturgical worship chanted by their canons and sung by their choirs. At their best they also remained centres of learning. This was what the Church of England later proudly boasted was an expression of its double nature: it was 'Catholic but Reformed'. Life in an English cathedral close after the Reformation might not have been readily recognizable, or acceptable, to those wedded to the old Catholic order, but it was nonetheless continuous. That continuity meant that not only were cathedral buildings maintained, but so too were essential elements in their chapters, in their liturgical worship and in their commitment to learning and teaching.

In England, Wales and Ireland the bishops who accepted the radical Tudor reform of the Church retained both their dioceses and their cathedral churches. Henry VIII's six new bishops (Westminster, Gloucester, Bristol, Peterborough, Oxford, and Chester) were given sees centred on what had been substantial monasteries and allotted a part of the dissolved abbeys' income. The old abbey churches were raised to cathedral rank and reconstituted with a chapter consisting of a dean and canons. The bishopric of Westminster was not to survive the accession of Mary I (though the royal abbey church was preserved) but the bishop of Oxford, who was never able to take full possession of the great abbey at Oseney, was finally obliged to use the chapel of Christ Church as his cathedral (Oseney Abbey has, alas, disappeared virtually without trace). When, in the nineteenth and early twentieth centuries, the Church of England woke up to the need for new bishoprics, yet again existing large medieval churches were called upon to serve as cathedrals (Manchester, Ripon, Southwell, Southwark and St Albans are the most memorable of these). They look for the most part as if they have always had the rank and architectural pretensions of an ancient cathedral. Only when parish churches in newly formed dioceses were deemed unworthy of assuming the dignity of a cathedral (Liverpool and Guildford, for example) were large Gothic churches constructed on new sites. With the revival of the Roman Catholic hierarchy in England and Wales in the 1850s, new titles were required as alternatives to those of the lost, and now Anglican, ancient bishoprics. Some of these titles had historic Catholic overtones (Westminster, Hexham and Menevia, for example) others decidedly did not (Clifton, Salford, Birmingham, Nottingham and Newcastle). In every case newly built cathedrals were required to serve the new sees. Most of these Catholic cathedrals had decidedly urban sites, often constricted ones and, however hard they tried, none of the first generation could be said to rival the finest churches of the Middle Ages which had been lost to the faith. Only with the advent of the great Byzantine-style cathedral at Westminster at the very end of the nineteenth century, and with the attempt to outdo the new Anglican cathedral at Liverpool with a gigantic domed Renaissance structure in the 1920s, did the relatively impoverished Roman Catholic Church in England claim its proper architectural dignity.

Since the late nineteenth century cathedrals have proliferated in England. New Anglican and Roman Catholic dioceses have either elevated the status of existing churches or made the bold and costly decision to build grand new ones. The Catholic cathedrals at Norwich (for the East Anglian diocese) and at Arundel (for the diocese of Arundel and Brighton), both of them formerly large parish churches, richly deserve their new dignity. A new cathedral at Guildford was constructed in the middle years of the twentieth century for the Anglican diocese founded in 1927, but elsewhere in the sees of Sheffield, Portsmouth, Bradford and Blackburn, older parish churches have been somewhat radically adapted to serve as bishops' churches and as the focus for their respective dioceses. The process of adaptation has not always been a happy one in architectural terms.

Other Episcopal churches now established in Britain have also acquired and adapted existing churches as cathedrals. Greek Orthodox cathedrals have been consecrated in London and Birmingham, and branches of the Russian Orthodox Church have designated two former Anglican churches in west London as cathedrals, richly transforming their interiors as proper settings for the Russian liturgy. Two of the most striking adaptations of existing churches are the reuse of the lovely, oval Classical parish church of All Saints at Newcastle-upon-Tyne (1786–96) as a cathedral for the Old Catholics and the acquisition by the Ukrainian Catholic Church of the former King's Weigh House Congregationalist Chapel in Duke Street, London, of 1889–91 (in its use of red brick and terracotta it is unmistakeably the work of the Victorian architect, Alfred Waterhouse). The old chapel is now designated the Cathedral of the Holy Family in Exile.

Regrettably, in a study of this kind there is no space for a long exploration of all the cathedral churches of Britain and Ireland, whether they be ancient or modern, whether they be of old foundation or of new adaptation. Therefore, I have necessarily limited myself to describing only Anglican and Roman Catholic cathedrals in England and have felt obliged to exclude the ancient and the modern cathedrals of Wales. The Anglican Church in Wales, now consisting of six dioceses, was formally separated from the Church of England in 1920 following disestablishment under the Welsh

Church Act of 1914. The Archbishopric of Wales, rather than being centred on a particular diocese, rotates between bishops who elect one of their number as primate (though, if historical precedent had been followed, it ought to have been the remote see of St David's that assumed the honour). Despite ruin and neglect over the centuries, two of the Welsh cathedrals, St David's and Llandaff, possess considerable aesthetic merit, yet even they would probably not figure prominently in any general survey of the greatest achievements of British church architecture. The ancient foundations at Bangor and St Asaph might strike a visitor as little more than large parish churches with little pretension to what is commonly assumed a cathedral ought to look like. The Roman Catholic cathedrals of the three Welsh dioceses that constitute a province of the still-united Church in England and Wales have, alas, little claim to beauty or distinction.

St David's Cathedral in west Wales nestles in a once-remote valley that conceals it from both the land and the sea, sheltering it from view as much as from Atlantic storms. This was where the ascetic St David centred his mission in the sixth century AD but the very seclusion of the spot seems to have proved something of an inconvenience to the later Norman bishops who aspired to erect a cathedral worthy both of the saint and of what they saw as their own episcopal dignity. David was formally canonized in c.1120, and it was decreed that two pilgrimages to his remote shrine were equal to one to distant Rome. Despite a steady stream of pilgrims and the rebuilding of the cathedral in the late twelfth century there could be no greater architectural contrast than with its contemporary, the great English cathedral at Durham. This, too, was erected in honour of a much revered, ascetic saint, but St Cuthbert's community had felt obliged to move from their original monastery, taking his relics with them. They were in search of a secure site, away from the sea and protected from the Viking raids that had also severely damaged the monastery at St David's. St David's Cathedral still modestly hides itself away, testifying to the saint's humility and desire for detachment from the world, the flesh and the Devil. For medieval pilgrims Durham Cathedral, on its hill above the River Wear, must have seemed to assert not the simplicity of St Cuthbert's earthly life, but his wonder-working afterlife. Here was the tomb of a saint in glory enshrined in a great church that also proclaimed the power of his successors as bishops. The histories of the two cathedrals and their bishops are revelatory. St David's was never a rich or influential diocese and by the sixteenth century, when pilgrimages were frowned upon, its first avowedly Protestant bishop was determined to transfer the see away from what he called 'a barbarous desolate corner' to the more populous Carmarthen. The cathedral's canons successfully resisted the idea but neglect, accentuated by a lack of resources, meant that by the late eighteenth century the church was a semi-ruin, with its choir cut off from the nave by a solid wall. Much of the structure that we have now is the result of a sensitive, but rigorous, Victorian restoration. The Bishops of Durham, by contrast, were powers in the land. Until the 1830s they were Prince-Bishops wielding a power which was both civil and ecclesiastical. Their cathedral and its chapter were also particularly well-endowed and though the great church was not left unscathed either by the Reformation or by the Cromwellian regime, it was kept in good repair. Such is its massive substance, its physical presence and the spiritual awe that it can inspire, it suggests to some that the many-towered Heavenly Jerusalem has descended to earth and established itself here on a Holy Mountain. St David's Cathedral recalls the humility of Christ the Servant. Durham Cathedral proclaims the Majesty of Christ in Glory. The architectural message they separately convey is not paradoxical. As living, working churches, rather than mere historical monuments, both in their different ways testify to the central Christian paradox: God Incarnate revealed himself both as the suffering servant and as Christ the King.

Andrew Sanders

1

THE MONASTIC CATHEDRALS

YOU CAN HAVE A bishop without a cathedral, but you cannot properly have a cathedral without a bishop. Despite the often loose use of the word 'cathedral' to describe any large church, the term has a specific definition and it is applied to churches great and small. Since ancient times bishops have been the elected chief pastors and teachers of Christian congregations. In their role as chief pastor, bishops have authority over a number of churches in a given district, and that district, which might cover a compact urban area or a vast tract of countryside, is known as the bishop's diocese or *see*. One particular church (the 'matrix ecclesia' or 'mother church') was selected as the centre of the bishop's activities and it was in this church that he placed his chair of office, a throne known as a *cathedra*. In this cathedra in the mother church of a diocese the bishop sat, in the manner of a Roman magistrate, as a teacher and instructor of those in his charge. The bishop's church was therefore his 'cathedral', the focus of his office as preacher and teacher, and the centre of his administration. In Spain, Portugal and their former colonies a cathedral church is often referred to simply as the *Sé*, a colloquial abbreviation of the Latin phrase *sedes episcopi*: (the 'bishop's seat').

The bishops of the early church tended to select established and populous cities as the centre of their pastoral activities. This explains why there are so many surviving bishops' sees in Italy. Once Christianity had made its impact on ancient society, virtually every Roman city had its bishop and the line of succession continues to this day, despite the fact that some of those ancient cities are now little more than small provincial towns. When the Roman Empire collapsed, however, size was not everything when it came to determining which cities would become the centre of dioceses. Venice, which was never an ancient Roman settlement, is still not technically a cathedral city. St Mark's is a basilica rather than a cathedral, and Venice's bishop properly has his throne in the church at Torcello. Even in Rome itself the early popes established themselves in what were once suburban churches rather than central ones. The Pope's cathedral is the great church of St John Lateran rather than St Peter's (which was, in ancient times, well outside the city walls).

Some commentators find it odd that the Archbishop of Canterbury, the Primate of All England, should have his Episcopal see in a Kentish city rather than in London. There is, as we shall see, an historical logic behind the fact, but there are even more striking anomalies in other European countries. London has a bishop rather than an archbishop, but not all capital cities, and particularly those cities that became capitals after the Middle Ages, were actually even bishops' sees. Berlin, for example, was little more than a market town until the seventeenth century and was served by parish churches rather than by an imposing Gothic cathedral. The Lutheran Church in Prussia, which did not have bishops until the nineteenth century, simply did not require a cathedral even though Berlin rapidly advanced to being one of the prime capital cities of Europe. Until recently Madrid, Warsaw and Budapest had no bishop of their own. All three cities had been belatedly selected as royal capitals in preference to their historical neighbours, Toledo, Gniezno and Esztergom, all of which were the venerable sees of the respective Primates of Spain, Poland and Hungary. Sometimes dioceses were moved to suit the ambitions of ambitious princes. When the status of Nancy was advanced to render it the handsome capital of the eighteenth-century duchy of Lorraine the diocese of Toul was effectively suppressed. The fine church at Toul, begun in the thirteenth century, was effectively left redundant when it was supplanted by a new baroque cathedral which was designed to be an eye-catcher in the elegantly planned centre of Nancy. The old cathedral at Toul retained its title, but was left without any elevated function beyond that of serving as an over-large parish church in a small French provincial town.

In the Eastern Orthodox Church the word 'cathedral' is used much more liberally than in the Western churches. In Russia, for example, a bishop designates several major churches, often in close proximity to one another, as his cathedrals. Orthodox cathedrals are found in monastic complexes, such as Mount Athos in Greece and in great fortresses, such as the Kremlin in Moscow.

The idea of having several bishops' churches clustered closely together was not common in the Western Church and certainly not in medieval England (even when the cathedral church was part of a large monastery). There are, however, seemingly glaring oddities in England's immediate neighbours. Even today in Ireland cathedrals seem to duplicate one another, while in Scotland large churches retain the name 'cathedral' but have no bishop serving in them. In Dublin there are two medieval cathedrals, both under the authority of the Church of Ireland's Archbishop of Dublin, while the Roman Catholic Archbishop of the same city makes do with a particularly handsome Neo-Classical church still known as the 'Pro-Cathedral' (though it is most unlikely that any future archbishop will ever build himself a finer church). Following the schisms and divisions of the Reformation, however, rival Irish bishops claimed equal jurisdiction. All of the medieval cathedrals were inherited by Protestant bishops and deans in the sixteenth century and generally remain in the hands of the Church of Ireland. Virtually all of the numerous Irish Catholic cathedrals date only from the nineteenth century.

In the Victorian period some Church of Ireland bishoprics were abolished by a British government intent on reform and diocesan funds were redistributed. In France a far more radical disruption took place. During the Revolution, sees were abolished or reorganized, leaving at least one superb medieval cathedral, Laon, without a bishop. This great church, which was once able to boast that its prelate ranked as the second most senior of the peers of France, now functions as a parish church. In Scotland, where the national church became Presbyterian in the sixteenth century and refused to accept the idea of bishops in its ecclesiastical organization, all of the ancient cathedrals lost their historic identity.

Some, like Elgin cathedral fell into ruin; others, like St Andrews, were deliberately blighted, leaving an impressive, if perpetually windswept, ruin. The great Gothic cathedral in Glasgow still rejoices in its historic title, but it was turned into two separate churches, serving two distinct Reformed congregations, in the sixteenth century. It was also purged of most of its medieval fittings and it now functions as a particularly magnificent parish kirk rather than as the seat of an archbishop. The Anglican and Catholic archbishops of Glasgow have modern Gothic churches elsewhere in the city. In Edinburgh St Giles's High Kirk is often accorded the honorific title of 'Cathedral' but it functioned as such only for two brief periods in the seventeenth century when the Episcopalian bishops of Edinburgh, imposed by the Stuarts, laid claim to it. Edinburgh now has a particularly fine nineteenth-century cathedral serving the Episcopalian diocese (St Mary's) and a rather less impressive church serving as the Roman Catholic cathedral (also St Mary's), but the handsome St Giles's is a cathedral only in name.

In England, cathedral life continued to develop both more steadily and conservatively. Only one major existing English building has lost its status as a bishop's church and that (surprisingly to many) is Westminster Abbey. The abbey's Benedictine monks were dispersed when Henry VIII suppressed the monastery. In 1540 the King raised the church to the rank of cathedral to serve a new diocese for the county of Middlesex. Having restored the Benedictine foundation, the Catholic Mary I suppressed the short-lived diocese in 1556. When Mary was, in her turn, succeeded by her Protestant half-sister, Elizabeth I, the monks were banished for a second time but the Abbey never saw another Bishop of Westminster. The territory of the diocese was reincorporated into the see of London. In 1559 the abbey church was made a 'royal peculiar', that is a church under the direct authority of the monarch rather than of a bishop. The Roman Catholic see of Westminster was not established until 1850, though its cathedral was not begun until some forty years later in a distinctive Byzantine style deliberately decided on in order not to compete with that of the Gothic abbey. Some tourists, it is said, assume that the abbey retains the title of cathedral. Others ask in vain to see the tomb of Mary, Queen of Scots, in the real Westminster Cathedral.

The survival of all the medieval cathedrals of England as func-
tioning bishops' churches is therefore remarkable, especially so
given the sometimes violent disruptions of the Reformation and
the subsequent suppression of the Church of England under Oliver
Cromwell's regime. Henry VIII not only retained the Catholic
dioceses which existed at the beginning of his reign, he created
six more (including the short-lived diocese of Westminster). At
Gloucester, Bristol, Peterborough, Oxford and Chester new bishops
were given large, and newly redundant, monastic churches as their
cathedrals. The formation of these new dioceses reflected both the
growth in England's population and the significance of the cities in
which they were established. Only in the case of Oxford was there
a somewhat awkward new arrangement. Here the bishop shared
a former nunnery church with Henry VIII's new college at Christ
Church. The cathedral's chapter is part of the college, and the
college's chapel also serves as the diocesan cathedral.

In early medieval times, however, established dioceses were not
so much suppressed as transferred. This meant that bishops moved
their sees either to larger towns or to more convenient administrative sites. They did not always have existing monastic churches to
move themselves into. Thus, the Bishopric of Crediton moved to
nearby Exeter in the reign of Edward the Confessor, while the ambitious new Norman bishop of Dorchester-on-Thames in Oxfordshire
decamped to the further end of his diocese and established a new
cathedral in Lincoln in 1072. Both of these cathedrals were what is
called 'secular'; that is they were run by canons in a chapter rather
than by monks. The East Anglian see of Norwich had originally
been established at North Elmham; it was removed to Thetford in
1075, before finally settling in Norwich twenty years later. All that
is left of Elmham Cathedral are the ruins of a parish church on a
low hill, and even these may not be the actual remains of the Saxon
church. Both Crediton and Dorchester Cathedrals were replaced
by singularly handsome medieval structures, the one a collegiate
church, the other an Augustinian abbey. But neither can now claim
to be a cathedral.

The most spectacular instance of a bishop moving his see is
that of Bishop Richard Poore of Salisbury. Of the once impressive

Norman cathedral of Old Sarum only foundations now remain. It had been established on a hill-top site on Salisbury plain in 1075 after a move from Sherborne in Dorset. The only evidence of its scale is its foundations, marked out in the chalk amid the sparse relics of a once mighty fortress. Old Sarum was abandoned by its clergy in 1218. The site was cramped, the water supply was restricted, and there were arguments between churchmen and their immediate neighbours, the pushy and disputatious knights who controlled the castle. With the Pope's permission, the Bishop of Sarum moved the centre of his diocese to a well-watered new site at Salisbury and began work on a singularly ambitious new church surrounded by a large close which provided ample accommodation for the cathedral's clergy. Bishops of Salisbury still sign themselves 'Sarum' but the bleak site of their former church speaks of little but change and decay.

The historic sites selected by the earliest English bishops for their cathedrals tell us a great deal about the early Christian history of the island of Britain. The fact that so many cathedrals seem to form an essential part of the living landscape of England also suggests the degree to which the church moulded both the fabric and the very nature of Englishness. When Christianity was estab-lished in the Roman Empire the province of Britannia had a church organized on the international model. Three British bishops were present at the Council of Arles in 314, but that integration of what was to become 'England' into the European fabric was lost when the first 'English', the Saxons, invaded. These pagan invaders not only brought a Teutonic polytheistic religion with them, they also drove Christianized Britons northwards and westwards out of the newly conquered territory. Any trace of Roman dioceses was lost. Romano-British settlements, including, we assume, their churches, were abandoned and destroyed. The invaders seem to have inherited a distaste for Roman cities and, in many cases, they seem to have left the ruins of those cities to further decay.

Only very gradually was a Christian presence re-established. Wales, where many Christianized Britons took refuge, remained cut off by its mountainous landscape, but there is impressive evidence of the civilizing influence of Celtic monks working as missionaries in the north of what was to become England. The major event in the wholesale re-conversion of the island was the arrival of the mission sent by Pope Gregory the Great from Rome in 597. According to the Venerable Bede (who had relatively little sympathy with what is often called 'Celtic Christianity'), Gregory had been particularly moved by seeing Anglo-Saxon slaves in Rome and had formed a resolution to convert their pagan homeland to the Roman discipline. As the immediate heir to the now crumbled Roman Empire, Pope Gregory was also anxious to restore its lost unity. In a sense he was determined to bring England back into the Roman, as much as the Christian, fold. As his chief agent in this enterprise Gregory selected a trusted protégé, Augustine, the Prior of the Benedictine monastery of St Andrew on the Caelian Hill in Rome. Augustine left Rome in 596, despaired of his mission while travelling through Gaul, but, encouraged by letters from Gregory, reached the shores of Kent by the following summer. Kent was at that time an independent Saxon kingdom with its royal capital at Canterbury. Here Augustine preached the Christian gospel to King Ethelbert. Augustine probably had the advantage of knowing that Ethelbert's queen, Bertha, had been born a Christian in Gaul and that she worshipped in a small church in her husband's capital. Ethelbert and his leading noblemen were evidently receptive potential converts. Ethelbert perhaps also recognized that conversion to Roman Christianity would link him and the kingdom of Kent to a wider comity of western European nations and ultimately to Rome itself. Having initially welcomed Augustine and his companions, Ethelbert was baptized and went on to encourage the wider mission in his kingdom. When Augustine was later consecrated as archbishop he naturally took Canterbury as his see. All of his successors as archbishop have been enthroned in a chair named after Augustine (though it does not date from Augustine's time) and presented with a venerable Latin manuscript of the Gospels which was probably integral to the original mission.

Augustine's arrival in Kent, and the establishment of Canterbury as his base signalled two things. Firstly, Roman Christianity would spread northwards and gradually supersede the less well-disciplined Celtic churches in the north of the island of Britain. Secondly, the example of Augustine's profession as a Benedictine monk would encourage the growth of monasteries at the core of the missionary work. Canterbury's cathedral would remain a Benedictine abbey until the time of the English Reformation. The same is true of Augustine's second foundation, the cathedral at Rochester, where the first bishop, Justus, had been sent from Rome in 601 to reinforce the mission.

The re-Christianization of Britain was neither straightforward nor untroubled. Augustine was not always tactful in his dealings with the Celtic Church, as Bede's account of his attempt to impose a Roman interpretation of ecclesiastical discipline and practice clearly shows. England was still divided up into a series of pagan Anglo-Saxon kingdoms and each responded to missionaries in different ways. Augustine's colleague Mellitus was consecrated bishop of London on the border of the kingdom of the East Saxons in 604. Here a new church, dedicated to St Paul, was built by Ethelbert to serve as Mellitus's cathedral. Ethelbert's successors, both in Kent and Essex were not always as sympathetic to the new religion as he had been and Mellitus was forced to take refuge in Gaul before returning to Britain in 619 when he became the third Archbishop of Canterbury in succession to Augustine and his successor Laurentius.

The foundation dates of these new English dioceses in the sixth and seventh centuries tell us of the gradual imposition of bishops who looked to Rome as the source of authority. Dorchester-on-Thames and later Winchester served the Kingdom of Wessex; Leicester, Lichfield, Hereford and Worcester served Mercia and its borderlands; while York, Ripon and Hexham were the first Northumbrian bishoprics. Surprising as it may seem, Sussex (the kingdom of the South Saxons), which was bordered by Kent to the east and Wessex to the west, resisted the process of Christianization longest. It was the energetic St Wilfred, briefly exiled from his northern diocese at York, who managed to found a diocese based at Selsey in 709 (later translated to Chichester). Bede tells us that there was a severe drought in Sussex but when the first Christian baptisms took place 'the rain, so long withheld, revisited the thirsty land'.

There had been a bishop of York in Roman times (he was one of the three British representatives at the Council of Arles in 314), but following the pagan invasions the diocese was not properly restored until the year 625. Paulinus, a Roman monk sent by Pope Gregory to reinforce Augustine's mission, went to northern England in the company of Ethelberga of Kent, who became the wife of King Edwin of Northumbria. Edwin seems to have readily accepted Christianity and founded a cathedral dedicated to St Peter at York. As was the case elsewhere in England, when Edwin was defeated in battle by a heathen rival, Northumbria reverted to paganism and Paulinus retreated with Queen Ethleberga to Kent (he later served as bishop of Rochester). In Paulinus's absence York seems to have been administered by Celtic bishops based at the monastery at Lindisfarne, but it was Wilfred, who became bishop in 664, who determinedly restored Roman usages and reintroduced Benedictine monks as missionaries. In 735, under Bishop Egbert, a member of the Northumbrian royal family, the Pope raised the status of the diocese to that of an archdiocese with a province stretching over the sprawling northern kingdom. Thus, by the mid-eighth century England had two archbishops, each with authority over their fellow bishops in their respective provinces and, moreover, a series of influential Benedictine monasteries, some of which harboured cathedral churches. Such was the confidence and pious zeal of the Anglo-Saxon monasteries in the early eighth century that it was they who sponsored the pioneering missions of two great English saints in Germany. For both men this meant a conscious return to the lands of their Teutonic ancestors, not as conquerors but as missionaries fired by the example of Augustine and his monks just over a century earlier. Winfrith of Crediton in Devon (better known as St Boniface) was to found the diocese of Mainz and the great monastery at Fulda before dying a martyr's death in Frisia in 754. Willibrord, a Northumbrian monk, also worked in Frisia but extended his mission as far as Denmark and the northern part of Germany. Having been appointed Archbishop of Frisia by Pope Sergius in 695, he was the founder of the diocese of Utrecht and of the great monastery at Echternach in Luxembourg. Willibrord died in the year 739.

The connection between the Benedictine abbeys and the development of English cathedral life is thus of prime importance. Though there is now only minimal architectural evidence of these monastic communities, the written evidence offers ample testimony to their vital significance in contemporary English life and culture. These communities were certainly of crucial importance to King Alfred's campaign to reconstitute Christian England after the assaults of the Danes. One particularly moving survival from the seventh century does, however, suggest something of the ambitions of the builders of the earliest English cathedrals. This is the crypt created by St Wilfred under the crossing at Ripon Minster. It is a structure of stark simplicity and of little inherent beauty, but the main, tunnel-vaulted chamber (which is only three metres long) suggests that Wilfred was well aware of Roman precedent. The crypt probably stood under the original high altar of a stone basilican church modelled on St Peter's in Rome. The rest of Wilfred's cathedral has disappeared, and the present church's status as a cathedral was only restored in 1836, but even as fragmentary evidence, the crypt at Ripon and a similar one at Hexham in Northumberland, indicate the ambitions of their founder. In a land of predominantly wooden secular structures these new stone-built churches speak of a deep sense that the new faith linked England both to the Roman past and the Western European present.

Given the systematic, and generally magnificent, rebuilding of the surviving cathedral churches by Norman and later bishops and abbots, it is virtually impossible to establish the proportions and pretensions of Anglo-Saxon minsters. Thorough archaeological examinations of what lies underneath our great cathedrals has been impossible. It was only when Winchester Cathedral was threatened with collapse in the early twentieth century, and York Minster in the late twentieth century, that anything like an exploration of more ancient subterranean evidence has proved feasible – and even then such researches have been precarious.

The magnificence of the Norman reconstruction of the Saxon cathedrals was a remarkable feat, both architecturally and in terms of their unprecedented scale. In the years immediately following the Conquest only one native English bishop remained in his see (Worcester). Not only were there new bishops; the heads of the greater abbeys were also supplanted by men of Norman origin. These were clerics who were possessed of a typically Norman imperial confidence – perhaps arrogance might be a better word.

However, their achievement, where it survives, continues to inspire awe. In their native province, cathedrals and abbeys had been recently constructed with elongated naves and in a noble style influenced by the civil basilicas of ancient Rome. The very scale of these great churches, such as the two abbeys that survive in Caen, were later to provoke the upper clergy in the Île de France to contemplate the rebuilding of the cathedrals in the dioceses of the Paris area. The new French-speaking hierarchy in England evidently found Saxon cathedrals unworthy of their status as pillars of the Norman kingdom. Their episcopal titles were continuous with the old order, but their cathedral churches needed to proclaim the innovative pretensions of the new. Work began at Canterbury in 1071, at Lincoln in 1072, at Chichester in 1075, at Winchester in 1079, at York and Rochester *c*.1080, at Ely in 1083, at Worcester in 1084, at old St Paul's in London in 1087 and at Durham in 1093.

FOUR MONASTIC FOUNDATIONS

DURHAM CATHEDRAL

There are fine, noble, and even extravagant Romanesque churches in France and Germany – one only has to think of Saint Etienne at Caen, of Saint Sernin at Toulouse, or of the cathedrals at Speyer and Worms – and there are dignified and impressive Norman naves in the English cathedrals at Gloucester, Peterborough and Ely, but there is no building of its time that properly rivals Durham Cathedral in splendour. The architecture of Durham is commonly, but justifiably, described in terms of superlatives. It stands on a promontory in a loop of the River Wear; below it, the river valley is wooded, but on its southern flank the city of Durham stands back from the cathedral as if in awe. The promontory also contains a handsome castle, once the preserve of the bishops, but now housing part of the city's university. Seen together, cathedral and castle give Durham a unique drama. At sunset, or early on a misty morning, or when castle and cathedral are floodlit at night, this drama seems almost contrived, like a fantasy image concocted by a Romantic painter. But the very sturdiness of the structures reminds us that they are substantial rather than ephemeral. The cathedral has three towers. The two pierced towers at the west end are contemporary with the Norman nave, but the great tower at the crossing dates only from the fourteenth century and has a supreme elegance which distinguishes it from its sturdy, square neighbours. Once all three were crowned with wooden spires. Yet even without these spires the long, shapely varied profile of the church remains uniquely impressive regardless of the angle from which we view it. From the east, the north and the south, it is memorably harmonious, but from the west, where the façade and the three towers appear crushed together when seen full frontally from South Street on the opposite bank of the River Wear, it can look all the more extraordinary.

Durham Cathedral was built on a particularly grand scale for three reasons. Firstly, its Norman bishops were considerable powers in the land and held the title of 'Prince Bishop', which gave them both civil and ecclesiastical authority over a great swathe of north-eastern England. They demanded a church worthy of their dignity. Secondly, the cathedral formed part of a great and prestigious abbey.

Durham Cathedral and Castle seen from Prebends' Bridge over the River Wear in this engraving after the watercolour by J.M.W. Turner.

26

Thirdly, and perhaps most significantly, it contained the shrine of one of England's most venerated saints: Cuthbert. Essentially, the cathedral is where it is and what it is because of Cuthbert. Cuthbert, who was a professed monk, had chosen to live as a hermit on the islands off the coast of Northumberland. He was renowned both for his sanctity and for his wisdom, and in 685 was chosen as Bishop of Lindisfarne with a jurisdiction over much of the north. When he died two years later he was buried in the monastery at Lindisfarne, but such was the honour accorded to his memory by his monks that he was exhumed in 697 and his body was found to be perfectly preserved. It was subsequently revered as a precious relic. When, in the ninth century, persistent Viking raids made monastic life at Lindisfarne perilous, the monks fled from their island, bearing with them Cuthbert's body. Two hundred years after his death the body was again found to be incorrupt. The monks wandered with their precious relic, establishing a community at Chester-le-Street which endured for a further century. Yet another Viking raid in 995 obliged them to move again and they finally settled in the much more easily defended site at Durham. Legend has it that Cuthbert's coffin became immovable and that the monks' prayers were answered by a vision of the saint instructing them that this site was to be his final resting place. Cuthbert's body still lies in a tomb behind the high altar in the new cathedral. The elaborate and costly shrine was dismantled at the time of the Reformation, but the depth of local piety seems to have been such that the much revered coffin was merely interred, with the body still inside it, rather than being destroyed (as proved to be the fate of the relics of most other English saints). Fragments of the Saxon coffin, and of the precious fabrics which once wrapped the saint's body, are preserved in the cathedral's museum. The pectoral cross, with four equal arms, which was found with the body in the 1820s, has since become closely identified both with the city and with its university. Thus Durham Cathedral uniquely honours its prime saint, but it also contains the tomb of another great and much honoured English saint: the Venerable Bede. Bede, the only Englishman mentioned in Dante's *Divine Comedy*, is the author of the indispensable first history of the island of Britain and of its Church. He is buried in the so-called Galilee Chapel at the west end of the church.

The surviving diocese and cathedral of Durham were founded in 998. Nothing of the incomplete Saxon church remains, for the incoming Norman bishops first built themselves a castle (1072) and then proceeded both to reform the Benedictine abbey and to reconstruct the cathedral on an extraordinarily ambitious scale. In 1092 Cuthbert's shrine was dismantled and the relics given temporary housing until a new church was ready to receive them. In 1104, after a series of architectural and financial vicissitudes, the vault over the high altar was completed and a new shrine was consecrated. The choir aisles were completed soon after and the nave opened in the early 1130s. The supremely elegant western 'Galilee' chapel was paid for by Bishop Hugh Le Puiset in the last half of the twelfth century.

The solidly satisfactory nature of the interior of Durham Cathedral is partly rooted in what seems to be the steady advance of its massive stone piers, variously decorated with incised zigzags, chevrons and chequers. The effect of these patterned columns when they were brightly coloured, as they seem to have been originally, must have been extraordinary. What might strike some modern visitors as an unrelievedly heavy interior is, however, enhanced still by the wonderful and highly innovative ribbed vault which rises above the piers and allows light to play along the length of the nave.

Despite the fact that Durham is so solidly an achievement of a great, if unknown, Romanesque architect, it is, like most English cathedrals, in fact, an amalgam of styles. The sometimes ponderous effect of the nave and the choir is transformed at the east end by the Chapel of the Nine Altars. This second transept is not a Lady Chapel (the Galilee functions as such). An unsupported legend has it that St Cuthbert proved to be such a misogynist after his death that any attempt to construct a Lady Chapel near his shrine was met with disapproval. In fact, the lie of the land at this point rendered a long eastward extension impossible. A well-buttressed lateral structure, lit by tall lancet windows, proved to be the answer. What the Chapel of the Nine Altars provided was ample space for the circulation of pilgrims to the saint's tomb and a series of altars available both for the display of relics and for the celebration of Mass by dedicated monastic chaplains. Uniquely, we know the name of the architect of this bold piece of planning, one Richard Farnham, and the name of a second mason (Thomas Moises) is recorded on one of the buttresses. Although the cathedral was grievously deprived of most of its medieval fittings both at the time of the Reformation and in the Cromwellian period, the joyfully spiky screen which separates the high altar from the saint's shrine happily survives. The screen was paid for by John, Lord Neville and now bears his name. It was made in London in 1380 of stone imported from Normandy, and it ripples with vertical energy as five major and four minor canopies rise up into pinnacles. It lacks its original sculptures, but its airy refinement renders this part of the cathedral dramatically distinct from the massively assertive piers of the nave.

The precincts of Durham Cathedral still retain many of the buildings crucial to the life of the long-lost monastery. The bishops lived in their castle to the north, an area separated from the church by Palace Green. The monastic buildings lay to the south in an area now known as the College (it still contains the houses of the canons, many of them bearing testimony to the extraordinary wealth of the eighteenth-century chapter). The largest house by far is the deanery, the former residence of the monastic prior. Of the community buildings there survive a cloister, a rebuilt chapter house and a fourteenth-century dormitory (which now serves as part of the cathedral library. Underneath the former dormitory is an earlier vaulted undercroft which is now divided up (part of it is the museum containing Cuthbert's coffin and the objects associated with it). The monastic kitchen, a vaulted square with great fireplaces on each wall, served, somewhat incongruously, as a bookshop. The former refectory above the cloister was converted into a library in the late seventeenth century. It houses a particularly rich collection of manuscripts and printed books and, despite considerable depredation, contains more books which survive from the monastic library than any other cathedral collection in England.

Durham, with its cathedral and castle on the hill, looks magnificent from the train. From the south the railway line emerges from a cutting and then, suddenly, there it is in all its splendour. From the north the view is less sudden, but as the train nears the city it is almost as dramatic. Otherwise, Durham hides itself modestly.

Ely Cathedral

Ely Cathedral cannot claim to be as modest as Durham. Ely can be seen from miles away, across the flat fens. It must ever have been so since the abbey at Ely was founded on an island surrounded by wild, watery marshland. St Etheldreda, a princess of the royal house of the East Angles, withdrew to this once-remote island for a life of prayer. She left for a dynastic marriage, but, yearning for monastic life, returned to the island *c.*672 as a professed nun. She then endowed a double monastery, for nuns and monks living in separate communities, but ruled over by an abbess (herself). The monastery had sovereignty over the isle and indeed until relatively recently 'The Isle of Ely' remained a separate administrative area outside Cambridgeshire. Etheldreda died in 679 and was buried, by her instruction, with her fellow nuns in a communal graveyard outside the church. Her reputation for saintliness was such, however, that the body was 'translated' to the abbey church as an object of pilgrimage. Etheldreda has two feast days: one marks her death (23 June) and her second her 'translation' (17 October). St Etheldreda's shrine was central to the life of the monastery at Ely until it was dismantled and the relics destroyed in 1538. An annual fair held in the saint's honour in October was once much frequented and the popular contraction of her name to 'Audrey' gave rise to the word 'tawdry' as a result of the cheap pilgrimage souvenirs and fabrics on display at the fair.

The shrine, the fair and the double monastery no longer survive. The double monastery had the shortest lifespan, being replaced by a solely male Benedictine abbey in 970. That in turn was suppressed at the time of the Reformation. The Anglo-Saxon abbey had its moment of celebrity when it was vigorously defended in a last-ditch stand against the Norman invaders by Hereward the Wake. This was the final act of military resistance to the new order. The 'Isle of Eels' (as the city's name indicates) had clear strategic advantages, for this remote hump of dry land was surrounded by an inhospitable fenland landscape crossed only by easily defended causeways. Hereward was defeated and the Conqueror ordered that the monastery should be plundered. The monks bought their way out of this threat for the sum of a thousand marks raised, it is said, by selling

The octagon of Ely Cathedral was built to the designs of Alan of Walsingham in 1328.

the church's treasures (though many of these same treasures were recovered within ten years).

So effective was Ely's recovery from this potential disaster that the Abbey was grandly rebuilt in the Norman style between *c.*1083 and 1130. In 1109 a new Bishopric of Ely was instituted, the diocese being carved out of the unwieldy see of Lincoln. The new bishop was the titular abbot of the monastery, though the administration of the community was devolved to a prior who also had responsibility for the repair of and extensions to the abbey church. The new bishops were often men of considerable substance, but the abbey too was rich, mainly thanks to the income from pilgrims to St Etheldreda's shrine. The particular grandeur of Ely Cathedral is thus partly due to its geographical setting and partly to the vision and ambition of its well-endowed medieval builders. Its long grey profile stretches along its island, relieved by a great west tower and its amazing central octagon. The cathedral has both a unique presence in the flat landscape of the Fens and an extraordinary architectural rhythm of its own.

Ely is sometimes fondly described as 'the Ship of the Fens', but it is a strangely unwieldy ship. Not quite a floundering galleon, more an absurdly top-heavy battleship of the 1900s – one built more for show than for battle. Ely Cathedral might seem like an Ark to some, but its shape is emphatically that of a great church. When the Norman building work was completed in the early twelfth century, the newly designated cathedral was graced by two great towers: one, which survives, was at the west end; the second loomed over the crossing. The sturdy Romanesque west tower is now crowned with an octagonal lantern flanked by four turrets, all of which were added in the early fourteenth century. The octagon was in its turn graced by a spire which disappeared only in 1801. It is this tower which determines the present profile of the church, but its octagonal crest also echoes the shape of a central octagon that spectacularly replaced the crossing tower in the early fourteen hundreds. The reason behind this dramatic alteration to Ely's original design was the sudden collapse of the tower on a February night in 1322. The monks had just left the church at the end of matins amid the gloom of an early winter morning. There appear to have been no fatalities but the damage to the cathedral was considerable. Not only was there a gaping hole in the middle of the structure, but three bays of the choir had also been destroyed. Once the nature of the catastrophe had been assessed an architect-engineer of genius emerged from the monastic community. This was Alan of Walsingham, the sub-prior and sacrist who had already designed Ely's distinctive Lady Chapel (which is virtually detached from the main body of the church). Alan turned the shocking, light-flooded scene of devastation into an extraordinary interior space. The lost tower was replaced not by a new tower but by an octagon. It took six years to build and entailed lopping off one bay each from the choir, nave and the two transepts, and forming an eight-sided area some 72 ft across. The eight new arched sides were rebuilt in stone by 1328, but above them rises a breathtakingly daring wooden structure – a lantern which is the Gothic equivalent of what later architects would deem to be a dome. (It may well be significant that the seventeenth-century Bishop of Ely was Matthew Wren, the uncle of the architect of St Paul's.) The lantern of the Ely octagon ingeniously employs the principle of the hammer-beam roof whereby raked, jutting beams of oak support a rising stage above. Although the whole invention must properly be ascribed to Alan of Walsingham, he seems to have been assisted by William Hurley, a master-carpenter associated with the King's Works in London. The interior effect is of a star-shaped space filled with light from the high windows in the lantern. Externally, the octagon and lantern are covered in lead but the effect is no less elegant and harmonious.

The cathedral and monastery of Ely were thus provided with a spectacular space in which ritual worship could take place. Both the choir, rebuilt in the Decorated style after the disaster, and the octagon were closed off from the nave by a screen or pulpitum, which was only removed in 1770. At the same time the monks' handsome stalls were moved eastward into the choir. The old arrangement had given the community an especially generous portion of the church in which the monastic offices could be sung. This pattern of monastic life and worship ended abruptly in 1539 when the abbey was surrendered to the King and the newly constituted cathedral was provided with a dean and chapter. The prior of the monastery became the first dean, but, having lost his titular position as abbot, the Bishop of Ely continued to occupy a stall in the choir rather than a throne. What was already a small diocese now had a giant cathedral church in what was effectively a small provincial town. With the loss of many of the temporal assets which had been tied to the monastery, and with the advent of the Protestant-minded Bishop Goodrich in 1541, the fabric of the cathedral began to suffer. The stained glass and all of the delicate sculptures showing the life and legends of the Virgin Mary were smashed in the Lady Chapel, and the chapel was reduced to the status of a parish church serving the town. The minster seems to have suffered relatively little damage during the Civil War, indeed, it is said that Cromwell himself protected it from further desecration by insisting that choir services be abandoned in order not to provoke his troops. Nevertheless, in 1699 the north-west corner of the north transept fell down and was rebuilt by a local architect. Such was the general deterioration of the fabric that in the middle of the eighteenth century a more gifted architect, James Essex, was called in to reinforce it. It was Essex who somewhat cruelly described the diocese of Ely as 'The Dead See'. Despite his unhappy and unscholarly rebuilding of the central lantern, and his ruthless re-organization of the interior (it was he who destroyed the pulpitum and moved the choir stalls), Essex probably saved the fabric as a whole. A further drastic 'restoration' was required in 1801, but much of the present state of Ely Cathedral is due to generally benign Victorian interventions. George Gilbert Scott not only refashioned the lantern above the octagon, thus restoring it to its original form, but also provided the cathedral with a remarkably good series of interior fittings (notably a new chancel screen, pulpit and reredos). Alas, Scott's decision to fill the upper canopies of the choir stalls with carved panels was more intrusive than happy. It was Scott who did what he could to restore the mutilated Lady Chapel, though it remained in use as a parish church until 1938.

Perhaps the most pleasing Victorian intervention within the body of the cathedral was the new nave roof. Where there had once been a roof open to the leads was transformed by a painted ceiling modelled on that at Hildesheim in Germany. The work was begun by Henry le Strange but was completed after le Strange's death in 1862 by the amateur artist and connoisseur, Thomas Gambier Parry (the father of the composer Sir Hubert Parry). The restoration of the roof under the tower had been undertaken in the mid-1840s by George Basevi, the architect-cousin of Benjamin Disraeli. Alas, while work was in progress, Basevi fell from the scaffolding, having stepped back, it is said, to admire his handiwork. He was killed by the fall – in his way a martyr to his art. Some critics believe that he might have gone on to be one of the finest classical architects of the Victorian era. Basevi was buried in the north choir-aisle, where a commemorative brass celebrates both his creative life and his untimely death in the service of a Gothic cathedral.

WINCHESTER CATHEDRAL

The great twelve-bay nave at Ely is one of the longest in England. That at Winchester is longer, consisting as it does of fourteen bays, helping to render it the longest cathedral in Europe. Unlike the surviving Norman nave at Ely, that at Winchester was transformed from a solid Romanesque statement into a far more delicate expression of the Perpendicular style at the very end of the fourteenth century by Winchester's most energetic and munificent bishop, William of Wykeham. William was not only a man of education and discrimination, he also appears to have been a gifted administrator with a self-evident love of architecture (he is accredited with the construction of the royal apartments at Windsor Castle). He acted both as Lord High Chancellor of England and, from 1367, as Bishop of Winchester, and in these offices he acted as founder both of Winchester College (1382) and of its sister institution the college 'of St Marie of Wynchestre', commonly known as New College in the University of Oxford (1379). Both the school and the college were built on an unprecedented scale and with the avowed intention of educating future generations of clergy and public servants (which were often the same thing). William of Wykeham is buried in a particularly impressive chantry chapel in the Perpendicular style which soars up to fill a bay on the south side of the nave. Although the Masses prescribed to be said in the chapel according to William's will have long ceased, the bishop's effigy is well preserved, having been protected during the Civil War by a former pupil at Winchester College. The chantry's desecrated interior was well restored in 1893 when new statues were inserted into the niches left empty thanks to the iconoclasm of the sixteenth and seventeenth centuries. This work was designed to commemorate the quincentenary of the school.

Bishops of Winchester have always been significant officers of state. Modern bishops remain prelates of the Order of the Garter and still retain their seats, by right, in the House of Lords (they rank with the Bishops of London and Durham immediately beneath the Archbishop of Canterbury and the Archbishop of York). In the Middle Ages the Bishops of Winchester commanded a particularly impressive income and the see was regarded as one of the most prestigious in Europe. The wealth of, and the honour accorded to, those pre-Reformation bishops is still evident in the sumptuous chantry chapels which help to make this one of the richest cathedral interiors in the land. The finest are those of Bishops Waynflete,

The nave of Winchester Cathedral was remodelled by William of Wykeham's architect, William Wynford, at the very end of the fourteenth century. The weight of Wynford's vault latterly added to the cathedral's structural problems.

Beaufort, Langton, Fox and Gardiner. These medieval prelates also left their mark on the city of Winchester. Their chief residence, Wolvesey Castle, now survives only as a ruin, but Wykeham's great school flourishes, as does the Hospital of St Cross, the oldest and certainly the grandest almshouse in England, founded in 1136 by Bishop Henry de Blois. Behind these institutions lay a charitable tradition which stretched back far beyond the first Norman bishops of Winchester (the first of whom was a relative of the Conqueror and the third, Henry de Blois, his grandson).

Winchester had dominated English secular life as the royal city of the kings of Wessex and later as the virtual capital of all England. It was also a city much frequented by the Norman and Plantagenet kings. According to a very dubious legend, the British king, Lucius, had founded a church here in 164, a church which was believed to have weathered both persecution under the Emperor Diocletian and the arrival of the pagan Saxons. What is infinitely more certain is that a significant church was established in the mid-seventh century by King Cenwalh of Wessex. It only became a cathedral church when the bishop of Wessex moved his see from Dorchester (in Oxfordshire) c.670. The Anglo-Saxon bishops of Winchester included the much venerated St Swithin (852–62) and the influential reformer, St Aethelwold (963–84). It was Aethelwold, a monk from Glastonbury, who introduced a community of Benedictine monks and who was determined to re-establish a tradition of learning and scholarship in the city. As at Ely, the monks were ruled by a prior, with the bishop serving as titular abbot. The cathedral, constructed by Aethelwold and his successor St Alphege, appears to have impressed contemporaries, though nothing of this early structure survives above ground level. The Saxon cathedral was certainly deemed to be splendid enough to provide a proper resting place for the body of St Swithin who had, like St Etheldreda, originally been buried outside the walls of the minster. A spell of singularly rainy weather in July struck some observers to be a sign of the humble saint's disapproval of this 'translation' from churchyard to church. This legend has also given rise to the popular belief that for forty days after Swithin's feast day in July the weather is either wet or dry according to its state on that particular day. Nevertheless, the shrine

The choir vault at Winchester Cathedral.

of St Swithin became a major focus of pilgrimage throughout the Middle Ages, the offerings left by these pilgrims adding considerably to the cathedral's coffers.

The Norman bishops began a wholesale rebuilding of the Saxon cathedral in 1079. This monumental Romanesque work remains visible in the transepts, but the long nave was gradually transformed in the Perpendicular style between 1394 and the early years of the sixteenth century. It was in this period that the nave was given a particularly elegant stone vault, the weight of which added to the structural problems which have steadily beset the church. The cathedral's original builders seem not to have selected the ideal site for their structure. The site slopes, and over the centuries the water table rose steadily. Underneath a layer of marshy peat there is indeed a solid gravel bed, but a decision had been made to lay tree trunks as a kind of raft and it was on this raft that the cathedral foundations rose. In time the raft sank into the marshy ground and much of the fabric was dislocated. Winchester Cathedral never boasted tall towers or spires, for it was recognized early on that they could not be supported. The crossing is crowned with a squat tower, but if, as some commentators have held, the original designers proposed six further towers (two at the west end, and one at each angle of the transepts), such ambitions were never realized. It was, however, at the eastern end of the church that an imminent collapse threatened in 1905. The cathedral's architects, advised by engineers, were obliged to underpin the fabric. This entailed sending divers down some fourteen feet into the watery peat in order to dig out the old log raft and to lay bags of cement and concrete in its stead. The water had then to be pumped out before bricklayers could construct proper foundations in the gravel layer. At the same time the south side of the nave was strengthened by supporting buttresses, designed to relieve the strain on the walls that had been imposed by the medieval stone vault.

Whether glimpsed from a distance or studied from Cathedral Close, Winchester has none of the soaring beauty of a Durham, an Ely, a Canterbury or even of nearby Salisbury. The emphasis here is on the horizontal rather than on a complementary vertical movement. Winchester Cathedral has also been shorn of the kind of monastic buildings which so enhance and enrich Durham. The zealously puritanical Bishop Horne demolished its cloisters, its chapter house and other buildings associated with the defunct monastery in 1570. The departure of the monks had rendered them redundant, it is true, but the demolitions seem to be occasioned both by Protestant antipathy to monasticism and, it was cruelly said, by a desire to save on their further upkeep.

The iconoclasts let loose at Winchester during the Reformation period also did considerable damage to the interior of the cathedral. Many of its fittings have been repaired, replaced or restored during the nineteenth and twentieth centuries but evidence of the destruction is not hard to find. Fragments of the superb sculptures from the fifteenth-century reredos are now displayed in the cathedral's treasury. Some of the damaged heads reveal an extraordinary observation and an exquisite sensitivity unrivalled elsewhere in England. In the eighteenth century the reredos was partly covered by a wooden altarpiece with the empty medieval niches above filled with Classical-style urns. In 1782 the Dean and Chapter purchased a painting of *The Raising of Lazarus* by the American-born artist Benjamin West, which continued to serve as an altarpiece until 1899 despite the fact that most of the sculptures had been replaced. The reredos as we now have it is a passable apology for the lost medieval masterpiece, but none of the tame sculptures has a jot of the liveliness of their irretrievably smashed predecessors. A once handsome seventeenth-century choir screen, designed by Inigo Jones and containing bronze statues of King James I and King Charles I, was dismantled in 1820. The royal statues (which had been buried during the Civil War) were displayed in niches in a new Gothic screen, but this in turn was replaced by a singularly unlovely structure designed by George Gilbert Scott in 1875. It is perhaps the least successful of all of Scott's often highly inventive church fittings that embellish a whole range of other English cathedrals. The handsome royal sculptures are now relegated to the nave of Winchester Cathedral and what remains of Jones's screen is preserved in the Archaeological Museum in the University of Cambridge.

CANTERBURY CATHEDRAL

Durham Cathedral was built to house the remains of St Cuthbert. The cathedrals of Ely and Winchester once proudly enshrined the tombs of their foundress and their greatest early bishop, respectively. Canterbury Cathedral was renowned throughout medieval Europe not for the honour accorded to its founder or to a Saxon saint, but because Archbishop Thomas à Becket was murdered within its walls in December 1170. Cuthbert, Ethedreda and Swithin had died holy deaths in their beds, but uniquely, Becket was acclaimed as a martyr and canonized soon after his brutal death. As the tracks called 'Pilgrims' Ways' in southern England, as chapels, hospitals and charities named after St Thomas, and, above all, Geoffrey Chaucer's *Canterbury Tales*, still suggest, a pilgrimage to Canterbury Cathedral was not only once integral to English life but was almost a definition of Englishness. That all ceased in 1538 when Henry VIII ordered the destruction of St Thomas's shrine and the elimination of his name from all ritual texts. A man who had died upholding the rights of the Church against the incursions of a king was not likely to be looked on in a favourable light by a tyrannical monarch determined to impose his own royal will on a newly defined National Church.

Though Becket's tomb has long disappeared, the cathedral at Canterbury remains just as much an elaborate shrine to the saint's memory as it is an archbishops' church. Beckett died in a substantial new Norman cathedral constructed immediately after the Conquest (1071–7). At the same time the Benedictine monastery which served the cathedral grew to become the largest in England and, in 1096, a new eastern arm was added to the church in order to provide a fitting setting for monastic worship. This new extension was raised on an extensive crypt which, being at ground level, is full of light. The new cathedral choir was consecrated with great ceremony in 1130, the kings of England and Scotland and every English bishop being in attendance. It was in this choir that the monks watched over Becket's mutilated body on the night following his murder

Canterbury Cathedral from the north showing the Central Tower, also known as Bell Harry and the Angel Tower, which was begun in 1496 to the designs of John Wastell. The south-west tower dates from the mid-fifteenth century but its companion to the north-west was rebuilt to a parallel design in 1833.

before it was ceremonially interred in the crypt. The new choir did not endure long for it was destroyed in a disastrous fire some four years after Becket's murder. The choir was sumptuously rebuilt by two architects, William of Sens and his successor William the Englishman, in the new Gothic style imported from France. When, in 1179, William of Sens was crippled by a fall from the scaffolding, the second William took charge of work on the supremely rich eastern extension of the choir, the Trinity Chapel and, beyond it the Corona. This area was always meant to house the relics of the martyred, and now canonized, Archbishop for it stood on the site of the chapel in which Thomas had said his last Mass. Becket's remains were translated here in 1220 accompanied in procession by Henry III and the primates of England and France. The Feast of the Translation was suppressed by royal injunction by Henry VIII in 1536. The Trinity Chapel remains a magnificent space, rich still in twelfth-century stained glass and graced with two significant Plantagenet tombs:, those of the Black Prince and of Henry IV and his queen. It was commonly rumoured that the usurping Henry IV had chosen to be buried here rather than close to the tomb of his cousin, Richard II, in Westminster Abbey, because he hoped for the intercession of St Thomas when the Last Trumpet sounded. The Black Prince and Henry IV now lack their sainted neighbour. Bereft of Becket's shrine the chapel still seems to have lost both its ancient focus and its spiritual and architectural logic. Nevertheless, the complex geometrical marble pavement laid down in front of the shrine still powerfully reminds one of what is lost. A tradition that the saint's body was secretly buried in the cathedral before the agents of Henry VIII arrived to destroy it seems to have no foundation. The 'secret' of the burial place was said to have been passed down by Benedictine monks evicted from the cathedral's monastery and retained through years of exile to be revealed only when England fully returned to the true Catholic faith. We still wait.

The architectural history of the eastern arm of Canterbury Cathedral depended, therefore, on two factors: the ritual needs of the monks and the presence of Becket's shrine. The circulation of the multiple pilgrims the shrine attracted also determined crucial aspects of the church's distinctive layout. Canterbury's complex architecture, as well as its surprisingly harmonious mixture of styles, are not atypical of English cathedrals, however. Relatively few English minsters have the architectural consistency of their French equivalents, but then French cathedrals tended not to be monastic. In France influential bishops, or particularly ambitious canons, rebuilt their churches over long periods but they generally remained loyal to an original aesthetic concept and to the founding principles of the design. English monastic cathedrals were reconstructed in a much more piecemeal manner, either because funds were ample at a certain juncture or because an aspiring bishop wanted to assert his status or his advanced taste. The demands of regular, communal worship of a monastery, as opposed to those of a secular chapter, determined the shape and the planning of the greater churches. Where pre-existing monastic buildings existed, the churches were often required to be integrated with them. At Canterbury there was an aggressive campaign of rebuilding of both church and monastery in the last years of the fourteenth century. The great cloister was reconstructed in the years 1390–1411, while the pre-existing and very substantial Chapter House on its east flank was given new traceried windows and a new hipped roof in the same period. It was in this Chapter House in 1935 that T. S. Eliot's celebration of the martyrdom of Thomas à Becket, *Murder in the Cathedral*, was first performed as part of that year's Canterbury Festival.

At Canterbury the monks' part of the church, raised on its crypt, was separated from the nave by a sturdy early fifteenth-century choir screen, or pulpitum, decorated with six statues of kings (being representations of kings rather than saints, they survived Reformation iconoclasm). The great vaulted nave, which replaced the Norman nave in the last years of the fourteenth century, is the work of the architect Henry Yevele (or Yeveley), an innovative genius who had worked both for the royal household and at Westminster Abbey. This hugely ambitious campaign to reconstruct the Norman western parts of the cathedral also entailed rebuilding the north transept, the hallowed site of Becket's murder. In this case at least, a desire for architectural uniformity seems to have supervened over both piety and sentimentality. Yevele's long, tall, supremely elegant nave is likely to strike latter-day visitors with an awe akin to that of their ancestors, but there is now no monk to greet them with a ritual sprinkling of holy water. The nave at Canterbury was much more than a particularly grand pilgrim reception area.

The body of the missionary church built on the site was almost

The magnificent nave of Canterbury Cathedral was reconstructed in the Perpendicular style in the late fourteenth century.

certainly inspired by the great basilicas of the Rome of Gregory the Great (buildings with which Gregory's missionary, Augustine, was very familiar). These basilicas were designed to hold large congregations as well as to proclaim the triumph of the Christian religion. When Archbishop Sudbury announced in 1377 that he intended to rebuild the nave, and called for subscriptions to fund the great enterprise, he was determined to make an architectural statement which would further Canterbury's status as England's prime church. Sudbury himself was murdered during the Peasant's Revolt (it was he who was blamed for the introduction of the Poll Tax and his unpopularity as a minister of the Crown was such that no one seems to have regarded him as worthy of a martyr's crown). Nevertheless, work on the western parts of the metropolitan cathedral proceeded steadily under his successors. The nave was completed by 1405. At its western end the south-west tower was rebuilt 1424–34, though the old Romanesque companion tower to the north of the façade was retained until it was rebuilt in a uniform style in the early nineteenth century. The seal was set on the late medieval reconstruction by the completion of a magnificent central tower *c.*1500, From a distance this superbly dignified crossing tower proclaims Canterbury's pre-eminence as an archbishop's church. Close up it reveals a luxuriance of detail held in check by the soaring upward accent. It is the work of John Wastell and was completed thanks to the considerable financial resources commanded by the archbishop, Cardinal Morton and the monastic community's prior, William Selling. The tower, known variously as Bell Harry and the Angel Tower, is unequalled in England for its utterly satisfying majesty, though some observers may recognize echoes of its proportions in the Victoria Tower of the Houses of Parliament in London.

THE PERPENDICULAR GENIUS

When the architectural writer and biographer of Henry Yevele, John Harvey, declared in 1978 that 'the Perpendicular Style is the most important phenomenon in English art', some of his more scrupulous readers might have balked. Harvey went on to explain that this last flowering of English medieval architecture was *'unique'* in Europe, its patterns being 'instantaneously recognizable [and] distinct to a degree unmatched elsewhere'. Harvey might be accused of special pleading, but lovers of English cathedrals know that he has a point. Victorian architectural theorists might have persuaded their discriminating contemporaries that the English Decorated style was the be-all and end-all of building design, while more recent critics have proclaimed the substantive qualities of the Romanesque and the chaste virtues of the Early English, but few were prepared to admit that the architectural achievements of the age of the last Plantagenets and the first Tudors had much intrinsic merit. These were, after all, the years marked by the bloody disruptions of the Wars of the Roses and by the religious decadence that was supposed to have been swept away by the impending Reformation. For much of the nineteenth century the predominantly Perpendicular parish churches of the West Country and of East Anglia were seen more in the light they threw on a regional prosperity based on the wool trade than they were regarded as light-filled, innovative masterpieces. The style was too often dismissed as repetitive and 'cold'. In 1966 Ian Nairn spoke of Eltham Palace in the outer suburbs of London as 'a perfect example of the innate heartlessness of much mid-fifteenth-century architecture, especially court architecture'. This memorable line struck the poet Geoffrey Hill so much that he quoted it in a preface to his sequence of poems called *Funeral Music* (1968). What may be true of the secular architecture of the 1450s is, however, far less valid when we turn from the castles, palaces and manors of the embattled Lancastrian and Yorkist aristocracy to the great churches built either by their ambitious clerical contemporaries or by those same aristocrats who were anxious to redeem their earthly sins by appeasing heaven. The great naves at Winchester and Canterbury, and the crossing towers at Durham, Worcester, Gloucester and, above all, Canterbury speak less of an 'innate heartlessness' than of a passionate aspiration.

2

THE MEDIEVAL SECULAR CATHEDRALS

In England, as much as in the rest of Europe, rivers mark boundaries and frontiers. Ancient English dioceses were often divided one from another by rivers, some of them major waterways, some little more than streams. It continues to puzzle many that the London metropolitan area is divided by the River Thames into two Anglican dioceses. North of the river, the Bishop of London has authority; south of it, his brother of Southwark takes over. The same division separates the Roman Catholic archdiocese of Westminster from the archdiocese of Southwark. The Anglican diocese of Southwark was only established in the first years of the twentieth century, but before that the area south of the Thames had historically formed part of the huge and wealthy diocese of Winchester before, briefly, coming under the authority of the Bishop of Rochester.

When Saint Augustine landed in Kent he had been given authority by Pope Gregory to establish two ecclesiastical provinces in Britain, both centred in prominent old Roman cities. One was to be in London and was to serve the southern part of the island; the other, in York, was to oversee the north. Early medieval archbishops of York were to assume that their authority stretched into Scotland, a presumption that was only abandoned when two new Scottish archbishoprics were founded in the fifteenth century. As we have seen, Augustine realized that, after the success of his mission in Kent, Canterbury was likely to prove a safer city for an archbishop's cathedral than London (a city then on the margins of Kent and surrounded by still heathen territory). The Primate of All England, therefore, still takes his title from the relatively small city of Canterbury rather than from the future capital city of England. Because the Thames once defined the northern boundaries of the kingdom of Kent, it also determined why Canterbury first became, and remained, a metropolitan see in a city that was always far from rivalling the real metropolis of Britain.

The episcopal cathedrals in London (established 604) and York (first tentatively established 627) are now radically different buildings in terms of their architecture, but they once had two highly significant things in common: both were 'secular' cathedrals (that is, neither was based in a monastery). Instead, both were administered by a body of priests who would later be called a 'chapter'. Secondly, both were probably built on the site of a pre-existing building dating from Roman times, the remains of which had survived the pagan invasions. If, as some historians assume, those buildings were old churches, the new cathedrals were 'restorations' of an old Roman order. More importantly, both churches were re-established in what would develop as urban areas. Being surrounded by streets, St Paul's in particular lacked the kind of cathedral close that would have rendered it detached from the city it served (unlike Salisbury or Wells, for example). Though York at one time possessed something akin to what we might describe as a 'close', it was gradually encroached upon. For centuries the western ends of both churches have been approached directly from populous streets rather than by means of a gate which separated it from the city. Like many French cathedrals both once had houses either built against their walls or hemming them in on two or three sides. When Sir Christopher Wren rebuilt St Paul's at the end of the seventeenth century he designed it to rise above the circumambient houses and shops and with a grand façade that faced, at an angle, directly onto Ludgate Hill. York Minster, which appears to have been founded on the site of a Roman fortress, still stands on firm ground safely above the areas so often flooded by the River Ouse, and it formed an integral part of the densely inhabited urban fabric of the medieval city that developed around it. As we see it now, the compact area facing York Minster's famously stately west front only came into being when houses were demolished in the 1860s. Its great southern flank was similarly exposed when Deangate was laid out in 1902.

DISASTERS ENDURED AND AVERTED

York Minster

The West Front of York Minster, from an engraving after J. Le Keux published in Britton's *History and Antiquities of the Metropolitical Church of York* (1819).

The great medieval St Paul's, once by far the largest cathedral in England, was lost for ever in the Great Fire of London in 1666. The destruction of old St Paul's means that York Minster can now claim the honour of being, in volume, the largest Gothic church in Britain. Completed in its present form in 1472, only Winchester exceeds it in length and Westminster Abbey in height. Its vast spaces and the supremely impressive impact it has on visitors sometimes serve to eclipse the fact that its history is both complex and replete with signal disasters. That it did not suffer the same fate as old St Paul's is due to two great and timely campaigns of rescue and subsequent restoration. The ambitious dimensions of the nave, choir and transepts are such that vaulting them in stone proved too daunting and expensive a task. The great vaults are consequently constructed of wood, and these great expanses of timber have thrice rendered the minster vulnerable to potentially catastrophic fires in recent times. On the night of 2 February 1829 one Jonathan Martin concealed himself behind a tomb in the north transept once Evensong was ended. In the locked, dark church he made a bonfire of prayer books and hassocks, allowing the fire to spread to the fine medieval carved choir stalls. It established itself in the organ case and from there moved up into the wooden choir vault. The roof was entirely destroyed, but the stained glass in the huge east window was saved with difficulty thanks to the efforts of the ill-equipped fire-fighters. Martin was arrested a few days later and tried at York Assizes. He was declared insane and confined to an asylum, where he died in 1838. The restoration of the choir roof was estimated to have cost some £65,000. Much of the money was raised by public subscription, with £5,000 worth of durable teak beams being provided by Navy Dockyards. Work on restoring the Choir was completed in 1832 but in May 1840 the nave roof suffered a similar fate, though this time as a result of an accident. The south-west tower was reduced to a shell and its bells destroyed.

The cathedral fortunately escaped major damage in the 'Baedeker' air-raid during the Second World War (its celebrated stained glass had already been carefully removed and stored), though the bombing wiped out several important buildings in the city. A major restoration, aimed at propping up the Minster's sagging foundations, had to be undertaken in the years 1967–72, but a major natural disaster struck yet again in 1984 when the south transept was hit by lightning. In the resultant conflagration yet another of the ancient timber vaults was almost completely destroyed. Modern visitors to York Minster may well be awed by the splendour of its architecture, by the extraordinary richness of its stained glass and by the quality of its monuments, but they need to be periodically reminded that these are particularly fortunate survivals. The nineteenth-century choir stalls are handsome enough and they blend in harmoniously with the minster's medieval fittings. Only the most discriminating of visitors is likely to regret that they do not have more antiquity. A considered glance up to the vaults and the enormous roof timbers above them should, however, suggest vulnerability rather than an enduring history. The upper parts of York Minster, as we see them today, are an ingenious and sympathetic twentieth-century re-creation arching across expansive medieval spaces below.

As the East Coast train sweeps south across the flat Vale of York, the tower of York Minster can be glimpsed from miles away. It is a squat tower, in many ways just a substantial stump which lacks the soaring elegance of those of Canterbury and Durham. The proportions of this tower are a consequence of the cathedral's weak foundations. In 1407, while work was proceeding on casing the old Norman piers at the crossing, the then existing crossing tower collapsed. Henry IV sent William Colchester, his master-mason from Westminster Abbey, to supervise a careful rebuilding. Even this skilled master was obliged to abandon plans for a much higher, two-stage bell tower (referred to as a 'campanile') probably because of concern with its foundations. It was the weight of this truncated tower, completed in 1472, which obliged the cathedral authorities to embark on the massive reinforcement of the foundations some five hundred years later. The excavations required for this undertaking in the 1970s did more than stabilize the huge structure above: they also revealed a great deal of important evidence of the long-lost Roman legionary fortress and of the substantial Norman cathedral built over it. Fascinatingly, however, very little was discovered which might tell us more about the wooden church established by Bishop Paulinus in 627 or of the stone Anglo-Saxon cathedral that existed until the Normans demolished it in the late eleventh century. Much is now made of the remains of the Roman city of Eboracum. Its one-time eminence is recalled in a re-erected column found beneath the minster and by a nearby modern statue of Constantine the Great, who was declared Emperor by his troops here in York 305. This belated tribute to the first Christian Emperor is a powerful reminder of what links York to a long Christian tradition. Not only was a bishop of the city present at the Council of Arles (which met some nine years after Constantine's accession to the imperial throne), but the current archbishop, like his predecessors, still formally signs himself 'Eboracensis'.

The structural problems which have periodically beset York Minster were not uncommon in the Middle Ages. In the centuries following the Reformation, English cathedrals, deprived of resources by Henry VIII, often endured the kind of physical neglect which eventually led to the threat of partial or complete collapse. At Hereford Cathedral in 1786 the fourteenth-century west tower imploded, bringing down with it the entire west end of the cathedral. Alas, given the late eighteenth-century's limited understanding of the Gothic style, such a devastating accident did not serve to inspire an architect of talent who might have turned such a disaster into an opportunity. In contemporary Germany or Austria it might have led to the imposition of a fantastic Rococo veneer; in France, a wholesale rebuilding programme in a new Classical style might well have been initiated. Instead, the penny-pinching Dean and Chapter of Hereford called on the services of James Wyatt (who had done such damage at Salisbury and Durham). Wyatt was an exceptionally talented Classical architect, but his facility with the medieval styles was limited. In order to economize Wyatt shortened the cathedral's nave by one bay, shaved off its triforium and removed the spire from the surviving central tower. Sadly, the western tower has never been replaced, but at least a worthy Gothic-style west façade, dating from the early years of the twentieth century, replaced the paltry apology for one left by Wyatt a century before.

Chichester Cathedral

Perhaps the most memorably well-recorded disaster is that which struck the cathedral at Chichester in 1861. Chichester Cathedral had been undergoing restoration work at the time and a grave weakness had been discovered in the piers supporting the crossing tower.

Chichester Cathedral after the collapse of the tower and spire in 1861, from a wood engraving from the *Illustrated London News*.

This thirteenth-century tower was crowned by a handsome spire which had been added in the fifteenth century. Masonry falling from the tower gave ample warning of the impending disaster, but shortly before half-past one on the afternoon of 21 February, in the middle of a great wind storm, the spire was seen to incline slightly to the south-west and then, as a contemporary source describes it, 'to descend perpendicularly into the church, as one telescope tube slides into another, the mass of the tower crumbling beneath it'. The fallen stones formed a great heap in the centre of the church, and the calamity struck some as resembling that which had befallen Ely Cathedral some five hundred and thirty years earlier. In 1861, however, the idea of an innovative architectural intervention, such as Ely's octagon, in such an historical structure proved unthinkable. The tower and spire were carefully rebuilt, in a manner closely resembling what had been destroyed, under the expert supervision of the architect Gilbert Scott. In the process Scott took the opportunity of heightening the tower by five feet, an alteration that offended some contemporary purists who complained that he had marred its historic proportions. The work took only five years to complete. The other major Victorian intrusion at Chichester, the rebuilding of the dilapidated north-west tower, took place in 1901.

Work on the reconstruction of the crossing at Chichester Cathedral, from a photograph of the 1860s.

As had happened at York, the cathedral at Chichester was first established amidst the ruins of a walled Roman settlement. The first Norman bishop, Stigand, transferred his see here from Selsey in 1075, taking over an entire quarter of the ancient city for his new cathedral and its ancillary buildings. The eleventh-century church may have been modest in size and architectural ambition, certainly if we compare it to York or Ely, but its later tower and spire serve to render it impressively monumental. In his section of the 'Pevsner' guide to the county of Sussex, first published in 1961, Ian Nairn sharply comments:

> A history of English medieval architecture could be written without mentioning any single part of Chichester, yet as a whole, it could never be left out ... Without any doubt it is one of the most lovable English cathedrals ... It is a well-worn, well-loved, comfortable fire-side chair of a cathedral.

This sense of well-tended intimacy has been conspicuously cultivated by Chichester's twentieth-century deans (notably Dean Hussey), who have happily introduced refined examples of Modern art and design. These works of art, which include a stained-glass window designed by Marc Chagall, a rather glaring John Piper tapestry behind the high altar and a beautiful *Noli Me Tangere* painting by Graham Sutherland, generally manage both to complement earlier fittings and to enhance aspects of the interior architecture. Above all, rather than intrude, as so many modern fittings do elsewhere in English cathedrals, they serve to open a dialogue with the most striking works of art at Chichester. These are the two superb Romanesque sculpted panels in the south aisle of the choir. One shows Christ approaching Bethany and the other the Raising of Lazarus. They may have once formed a part of the long-demolished twelfth-century choir screen, but were found intact in 1829 hidden behind the choir stalls. Shorn of their original context, but wonderfully preserved from the malevolence of sixteenth-century iconoclasts, they have a stark drama which is expressed in the vigour of faces and gestures and in the massive folds of the drapery. Despite Ian Nairn's comparison of Chichester Cathedral to a domestic fireside, these panels are a long way from being 'comfortable'.

SALISBURY CATHEDRAL

Chichester Cathedral sits superbly both in the context of the city surrounding it and in the broad landscape of East Sussex. Its spire forms a memorable landmark and, uniquely amongst English cathedrals, it is also a sea-mark, for the land to its south stretches out flatly towards the English Channel. Despite the undoubted elegance of Chichester's steeple, it cannot claim to rival the memorable beauty of the spire of Salisbury Cathedral. It, too, totally and happily dominates its urban and rural setting. Salisbury's spire is one of the wonders of England. It has a matchless, shapely refinement whether it is steadily viewed during a walk across the nearby water-meadows, or it is studied close at hand or directly from below, piercing the sky above the cathedral's cloisters. The Salisbury spire has *presence*. In the eyes and minds of its original early-fourteenth-century builders that presence was enhanced by a relic of the Blessed Virgin Mary's girdle, which had been lovingly placed in a small box at the apex of the steeple.

The American novelist, Henry James, somehow irritated by perfection, complained in his book of essays called *English Hours* that the spire was 'banal' and that the 'sweet perfection' of the cathedral's west front would eventually make him weary. 'There are people by temperament easily sated with beauties specifically fair,' he wrote, 'and the effect of Salisbury Cathedral architecturally is the equivalent to that of flaxen hair and blue eyes physiognomically.'

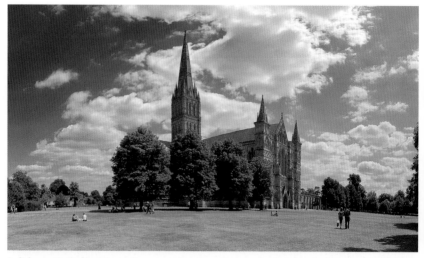

Salisbury Cathedral from the west showing its extensive close. A detached bell-tower, which stood on the north side of the cathedral, was demolished by James Wyatt in 1790.

James doesn't disagree with the idea that Salisbury is a 'perfect specimen' of what an English minster ought to be; he just finds it *too* perfect, *too* 'nice'. Like other denigrators he was disinclined to let English art be represented by anything so shapely, so tidy, so obviously harmonious. Such denigrators tend to want Englishness to be expressed by something more untidy, more rugged or more sinuous; by something wittier, even something less obtrusive or less obvious. They are all wrong, of course.

In truth, Salisbury Cathedral is not perfect. The wonderful fourteenth-century tower and spire do not really fit onto the thirteenth-century body of the church and, it must be admitted, the cathedral's west front with its commonplace nineteenth-century sculptures is clumsy and could not remotely be compared in beauty to those of Rheims, Chartres or Amiens in France. Nevertheless, the close surrounding Salisbury Cathedral is a wonder, not because of its medieval buildings, but because it was fortunate to be redeveloped by a series of talented jobbing architects in the late seventeenth century. The cathedral now rises from uncluttered green lawns only because the lumpy, detached bell-tower, which once stood to the south of the nave, was demolished in 1790. The architect who was to blame for that demolition, James Wyatt, also destroyed two chantry chapels at the east end of the church and either swept away, or moved, many of the cathedral's best internal fittings. He did so in the name of order. Constricted by the prejudices of his age, Wyatt wanted Gothic architecture to be both romantic and unnaturally tidy. His work at Salisbury, in the name of 'improvement' can only be described as mutilation, and it is small wonder that the impassioned nineteenth-century critic and architect, A.W.N. Pugin characterized him as 'Wyatt the Destroyer'.

The mid-thirteenth-century nave of Salisbury Cathedral was left 'uncluttered' by James Wyatt in the late eighteenth century, and again by the mid-twentieth century Dean and Chapter.

Alas, Wyatt's mission to impose an antithetical new order on the cool, rhythmical beauty of the interior of Salisbury Cathedral has continued into the modern era. Wyatt also demolished a solid medieval choir screen and replaced it with a gimcrack affair made up of fragments of the chantries he had knocked down. That screen was in turn removed by Sir Gilbert Scott in the 1870s and replaced by an elaborate and inventive open-work metal screen. Scott also added a substantial stone reredos which once properly separated the choir from the retro-choir. Scott's work was deemed to be both ugly and inappropriate by a particularly philistine dean and chapter and both the magnificent screen and the less dramatic reredos were summarily disposed of in 1960. That dean, like Wyatt, was acting in the name of opening up an uncluttered grand 'vista' from west

The new high altar of Salisbury Cathedral, with the exposed view of the retro-choir and Lady Chapel behind it, goes against what the cathedral's medieval builders would probably have demanded.

to east, but such vistas are utterly alien to the medieval concept of a working cathedral church. In 2008 work began on re-cluttering the nave with a newly designed marble 'font', a dribbling elephantine water feature singularly out of place here and unworthy of its exquisite setting. After two hundred years the work of Wyatt 'the Destroyer' has a fresh context. Present-day lovers of Durham Cathedral still breathe sighs of relief that Wyatt's scheme to enact a similar 'tidying up' there was aborted. Alas, the appropriate lessons seem not to have been learned at Salisbury.

The fabric of the cathedral at Salisbury may have required periodic and radical restorations (such as Gilbert Scott's in the years 1865–78). These overhauls saved Salisbury from the signal indignity of a structural collapse akin to Chichester's or the ones threatened at Winchester in the early twentieth century and at York in the 1960s. Admittedly, the inspired builders of Salisbury's spire realized that the weight of the new tower required the insertion of strainer arches in the eastern transept, but otherwise the church was fortunate to possess well-laid and secure foundations. It is very possible that the collapse of the tower at Ely, and the steady sinking of Winchester's eastern chapels, were the result of decisions made too hastily when the cathedrals were rebuilt by overly ambitious and probably impetuous Norman bishops in the eleventh century. Salisbury Cathedral was 'purpose-built' on a new, carefully selected site from 1220 onwards. The diocese was once served by a substantial, but not huge, Norman cathedral, but this was some miles away at a site now known as Old Sarum. The see had moved twice before it ended up in Sarum in 1075 (the diocese was first centred in Ramsbury in Wiltshire, and then at Sherborne in Dorset). Looking at the scanty remains of Old Sarum now, it is difficult to credit the decree of the Council of Windsor issued in the year 1075 that cathedrals should be moved from obscure towns to places of greater note. Sarum was a garrison town, formidably defended, but windy and waterless. By the early twelfth century the clergy were beginning to find their situation cramped, both in terms of the cathedral's limited site and because of the annoyance of living cheek-by-jowl with a dominant soldiery. As a consequence Bishop Richard Poore and his chapter resolved to move their church down from the chalk uplands to a well-watered, but

The late thirteenth-century cloisters of Salisbury Cathedral are the largest in England.

well-drained site on fertile meadowland below. Even today Salisbury Plain is the preserve of soldiers, but Old Sarum and its former fortress have long since virtually vanished (though scandalously it still sent an MP to Westminster until the Reform Act of 1832). It was said that Bishop Poore had been vouchsafed a vision from the Virgin Mary herself telling where to begin his new church which would be dedicated in her honour. He thus had a 'Virgin' site in both senses of the term. The foundation stone of the new cathedral was laid in April

1220. The new, planned city of Salisbury received a Royal Charter seven years later, and the cathedral and its ancillary buildings, which lie at the heart of it, were completed by 1266. Work on the tower and spire did not begin until forty years later.

Salisbury Cathedral is situated in a very substantial walled and gated close. When this wall was constructed in 1331 the canons who made up the chapter were ordered to build themselves permanent

The chapter house of Salisbury Cathedral was built in the second half of the thirteenth century.

stone dwellings using redundant masonry from the abandoned site at Old Sarum. Of all English cathedrals Salisbury is the most emphatically a secular as opposed to a former monastic establishment. Nevertheless, the canons added certain features adjacent to their church which we might at first sight associate with a monastery. They constructed a spacious and singularly beautiful vaulted cloister to the south-west.

Despite the absence of monks, this was, and remains, the largest cloister in England. On the eastern arm of this cloister the canons built an octagonal chapter house in which to transact their daily business. Though it required a rigorous restoration in the middle years of the nineteenth century, during which its intricate sculptural scheme was well-repaired and its large traceried windows re-glazed, this chapter house with its great central pillar remains a majestic space. Like the tower and spire, the cloister and the chapter house form a superb complement to the rich Early English style of the cathedral. Uncluttered by the ancillary buildings of a monastery (refectory, dormitory, etc.) Salisbury Cathedral in its generous and distinguished close retains the kind of perfection which might have troubled the punctilious Henry James but which, in the eyes of less prejudiced observers, has always rendered it one of the true glories of Britain.

THE SECULAR CATHEDRAL AS A COMMUNITY

Lincoln Cathedral

Salisbury Cathedral and its close were famously depicted both in sunlight and threatened by dark storm clouds in a succession of paintings by John Constable (a close friend of one of its canons). Constable seems to have associated the rough weather he sometimes portrayed with threats to the general well-being of the contemporary Church of England. Salisbury, serene amidst the water-meadows despite the black clouds and odd streaks of lightning, stands for something enduring. The distant view of Lincoln Cathedral across the flat lands of Lincolnshire suggests something very different. It

Wenceslas Hollar's engraving of Lincoln Cathedral from the west shows the surviving spires on the western towers (from Sir William Dugdale's *Monasticon Anglicanum* (1672)).

is no less serene and enduring, but this cathedral asserts something which is at the same time transcendent and triumphant. Lincoln, like Durham, with its three towers is magnificent and conspicuous. It must have been even more so when those towers were capped with timber and lead spires. The great central spire was destroyed in 1548; those on the western towers disappeared only in 1807.

The first cathedral on the site had proved particularly prone to disaster. Lincoln became the centre of a large diocese only in 1072 when William the Conqueror instructed Bishop Remigius of Dorchester-on-Thames to move his cathedral here. With the assent of the Pope and of the Archbishop of Canterbury (in whose province the see lay), a new church was built on a hill-top site just to the east of the newly established Norman garrison at Lincoln Castle (although the church's dimensions were restricted by the city wall). Yet again an old Roman settlement had become a stronghold of the new military and ecclesiastical order – an order guarded by strong walls which aimed to awe its Anglo-Saxon subjects into political and cultural submission. The plan of Remigius's church appears to have been based on that of Canterbury. It had a long nave, a central tower and a eastern apse. Two western towers were added in the early years of the twelfth century. In 1141 the cathedral's roof was destroyed by fire and in April 1185 a severe earthquake seriously damaged the rest of the fabric, utterly demolishing the central tower and splitting the minster 'from top to bottom'. It has been argued that this collapse was less the result of the earthquake than of faulty construction. Nevertheless, the disaster gave the new bishop, Hugh of Avalon (a Burgundian by birth and a Carthusian monk by profession), a proper excuse to begin the task of an elaborate rebuild in the new Gothic style. As a consequence of Hugh's initiative, Lincoln Cathedral was gradually reconstructed between 1192 and 1280. Hugh also opened the door to a radical stylistic re-think of the nature of his church. Though much of the new cathedral was completed after his death (Hugh died in 1200 and was canonized in 1220), it was his new eastern arm, which is now generally called 'St Hugh's Choir', that established the grand proportions of the new church. Moreover, it determined the leading stylistic principles on which the great minster would be developed. The superb consistency and richness of the architecture of the new church makes it one of the very finest achievements of medieval Christianity.

The transformation of Lincoln in the years after Hugh's death was given a new incentive by the bishop's canonization. Subscribers to the continuing building campaign were enrolled in a sodality for whom prayers were said at the saint's tomb. Hugh had lived a conspicuously holy life during his time in office, retiring annually to the Carthusian priory he had established at Witham in Somerset, but such was the reverence in which he was held after his death that his shrine in Lincoln Cathedral was second only to that of Thomas à Becket in attracting pilgrims. When his body was moved to a rich new shrine in the eastern part of the Angel Choir in October 1280, the ceremony was attended by Edward I and his wife, Eleanor, the Archbishop of Canterbury, and eight other bishops. Alas, St Hugh's shrine was systematically despoiled by Henry VIII's commissioners in 1542 and no trace of it remains in the present cathedral.

Lincoln Cathedral from the north-east showing its spectacular position dominating the city and the surrounding wolds.

Ironically, what does survive is the base of a second shrine, that of 'Little St Hugh', a Christian child supposedly ritually murdered by Jews in 1255 (the story is properly described as 'trumped up' by the present cathedral authorities, but its unhappy contemporary resonances are reflected in Chaucer's 'Prioress's Tale').

If one requires a fitting monument to St Hugh it is the cathedral itself. Although the saint-bishop was a man whose life embodied Carthusian austerity the architecture he inspired is complex, noble and almost sumptuous. The work of Hugh's unknown master-builder combines audacity with a rationale that at times appears perverse. The arcading of the choir is regular, with rising shafts of black marble that contrast with the mellow cream of the stone. Above this regular rhythm of piers and arches soars a high vault which has been characterized as 'crazy'. It is certainly unlike the comparatively 'conventional' vaulting in contemporary French cathedrals. Lincoln's choir vault does not so much break rules as re-think them. The vault seems perversely to ignore the bays below. Ribs appear to branch out randomly, with one particular rib springing from the marble shafts and shooting diagonally into the neighbouring bay rather than, as architectural convention might demand, terminating in a central boss. Instead of forming a neatly conventional quadripartite pattern, everything seems at first sight to be askew. Nevertheless, there is a clear structural and aesthetic logic at work here. The vault may at first sight seem disconcerting, but a more steady contemplation suggests that what is actually happening above our heads is a singularly happy example of daring inventiveness. English Gothic architecture can push structural rules to their limits in a way that resembles the most playful aspects of the seventeenth-century Baroque. The choir at Lincoln is a case in point.

St Hugh's successors extended his choir eastwards, a scheme that required the demolition of part of the inconvenient city wall, but which provided ample space both for the saint's shrine and for the movement of pilgrims to it. This bold extension, known as the 'Angel Choir', came to fruition under Bishop Robert Grosseteste (1235–53). Although St Hugh's new central tower collapsed in the late 1230s, work on transforming the western parts also proceeded apace. A glorious new nave was begun in the early 1230s. This nave follows the principles of design established in the choir, though with far more conventional vaults. The superb main transepts contain to the north the complex rose window known as 'the Dean's Eye' which rises above a row of seven lancet windows. It is paralleled in the south transept by the fourteenth-century window styled 'the Bishop's Eye'. Despite this long-drawn-out programme of construction, and an equally long succession of gifted master-builders, Lincoln Cathedral possesses an architectural consistency rivalled only by that of Salisbury.

Like Salisbury, Lincoln is fortunate to retain a number of ancillary buildings connected to its dean and chapter. Its cloisters may have been disappointingly subjected to a series of restorations, but the decagonal Chapter House, approached, as at Salisbury, by a vaulted passage, wonderfully complements both the internal vaults of the church and its external bulk. The north side of the cloister was replaced in the late seventeenth century by a new library, designed by Sir Christopher Wren. The Library, built on the principles of a college library, shows Wren at his most modest

Lincoln Cathedral from the south-east showing its crossing tower, which was heightened 1307–11. The cathedral's lead spire was blown down in 1548.

and undemonstrative. Indeed, it is so modest that it is often passed over in surveys of the architect's work. It nonetheless serves to enhance the happy distinctiveness of that beacon of civilization: the uniquely ravishing architectural ensemble which crowns the hilltop at Lincoln.

WELLS CATHEDRAL

Although they may be paralleled by structures which once served the monks in the former monastic cathedrals of England, the libraries, cloisters and chapter houses of the medieval secular cathedrals powerfully remind us of the prestige and learning which were once fostered by the clergy who ministered in them. Cathedral chapters were at the centre of communities of well-educated men and boys, who lived apart from the busy life of the cities that surrounded their churches. The canons, their assistant priests, their lay-clerks and their choristers led ordered lives; they were well housed, and the steady pattern of their communal worship took place in spaces of unequalled splendour. Certainly, very few other buildings in English cathedral cities could ever have rivalled the towering glory of the minsters which generally formed the core of the religious life of many of those cities. London, York, Norwich and medieval Lincoln were influential commercial centres, but even in those cities few secular buildings were likely to have approached the comforts, the sanitation and, above all, the security of a cathedral close.

Wells in Somerset still exhibits a series of remarkably impressive reminders of the well-endowed ecclesiastical establishment that served and maintained the life of the cathedral church. Wells is a small city. It was probably never particularly large, even in terms of the relatively small populations of other English towns in the medieval period. The fact that the diocese of Wells shares its title with the rather larger city of Bath suggests the importance accorded to that ancient Roman settlement. Not only did the cathedral at Wells have Bath Abbey as a fellow claimant of its bishop's title, it was also situated close to one of the most venerable monasteries of England: Glastonbury. The abbots of Glastonbury proudly insisted that their church had been founded in the first century by none other than Joseph of Arimathea, and that Joseph had brought the Holy Grail with him to Somerset. These probably mythical associations certainly added to the mystique attached to Glastonbury. Blessedly, the fine quality, and the mellow hue of the local stone meant that all three religious communities constructed particularly fine churches. Whatever the historic rivalry that existed among Wells, Bath and Glastonbury, Wells must always have been able to hold its own both as the bishop's principal church and, moreover, as a cathedral which ranks amongst the most satisfyingly beautiful in the land. Glastonbury Abbey now survives only as an extensive but sad ruin, while Bath Abbey (which has never claimed to be a 'co-cathedral') was rebuilt in a singularly repetitive Perpendicular style in the last years of pre-Reformation England. Wells's architectural supremacy in its region is now unrivalled.

As in its medieval heyday, modern visitors to Wells approach its cathedral through a gatehouse which suddenly opens up onto a spacious lawn from which the western façade of the church rises abruptly. The important ancillary buildings attached to the cathedral – the cloister, the chapter house, the accommodation provided

The nineteenth-century stone canopies added to the choir stalls at Wells Cathedral.

69

for the vicars' choral and the memorable Bishop's Palace – are either invisible or secondary to the immediate impression made by this great west front. This dominant façade is effectively a screen decorated with a dense array of sculpture. These sculptures were once gorgeously painted, evidence of the extravagant brightness which was revealed when the façade was carefully cleaned and restored in the years 1974–86. The effect now may be largely monotone, but the golden stone is relieved with shafts of darker marble and, given an interplay of sunlight and shadow, it possesses a stately elegance. Above this screen rise two towers: one built in the late fourteenth century; the other, closely resembling it, in the early fifteenth century. These towers have the air of being cut off in their prime for, unlike the great central tower, they end in a low parapet and a little frilly decoration. The pinnacles were probably intended to rise higher, or they may have supported spires which, sadly, were never constructed. In the absence of a surviving plan or evidence in the stonework, no subsequent architect has dared to impose his designs on the upper stages of these towers. Nevertheless, compared to the many gloriously inventive steeples that adorn the parish churches of the diocese these are a mild disappointment.

The word 'disappointment', however, could never properly be applied to the interior of Wells Cathedral. It is sublimely beautiful in its architectural rhythms. Wells may lack the height and length of Lincoln or Salisbury, and its indulgent breadth renders it utterly distinct from the vertical emphasis of contemporary French churches, but the twelfth-century architect of the western part of Wells had complete confidence in the distinctive richness of his art. Since the 1330s the nave has culminated in a great scissor arch formed out of one pointed Gothic arch surmounted by another inverted Gothic arch. There are huge, circular eyes in the spandrels which add to the striking magnificence and individuality of the effect. This strainer arch, and its three neighbours to the east, south and north, were inserted to relieve the considerable downward pressure imposed by the new central tower. The scissor-shaped arches are not a unique invention (there are parallels in Bristol Cathedral and slightly more awkward examples in the transepts at Salisbury), but at Wells they have a special elegance. It is often fondly claimed that the arches

The great strainer arch at the east end of the nave at Wells Cathedral. The early twentieth-century rood figures stand on the original medieval soffits.

honour the X-shaped cross – the saltire – the traditional symbol of the cathedral's patron saint, St Andrew. When in the 1920s a rood and statues of the Virgin Mary and St John were replaced on the sockets that had survived Reformation iconoclasm the immense scissor of the westernmost arch took on a renewed symbolic and liturgical function. It both divides the nave from the crossing, with the tower vault beyond it, and it seems to introduce us to the thrilling view that lies to the east.

71

The true genius of the anonymous architects of Wells Cathedral is revealed in the complex vaulting of the choir and retro-choir and in the Lady Chapel beyond them. These wonderful spaces date from c.1285–1340 and possess a dazzling inventiveness, but their design never lacks a deeply satisfying logic. When he offered an especially detailed analysis of the vaulting system in the eastern chapel at Wells, Nikolaus Pevsner rightly felt inspired to compare this incomparable achievement of the English Decorated style to the intricate wonders of the eighteenth-century German Rococo. The German connection runs deep. Scholars have long argued that the vaulting systems pioneered by English master-builders in the fourteenth century were readily adopted by their German and Bohemian contemporaries and then developed into even suppler forms. It is at Wells and at nearby Bristol that we can first recognize the beauty of a vault that springs from a stem like a lush young plant unwinding its fronds before spreading out into regular star-like formations. The ultimate triumph of the Wells vaulting systems is the roof of the octagonal chapter house. This chapter house, which is raised up on a vaulted undercroft, has a central pier from which spring no fewer than thirty-six ribs (the comparable chapter house at Westminster Abbey has sixteen ribs; that at Lincoln twenty). At Wells, five clustered wall-shafts support the vault from the angles between the windows. It is a magnificent space made even more memorable by the approach to it up a curving staircase worn into its uneven state by the feet of ancestral visitors.

Apart from its romantically moated Bishop's Palace and the nearby fifteenth-century Deanery, the most extraordinary of the cathedral's ancillary buildings is the so-called Vicars' Close. This contained the quarters provided in the mid-fourteenth century for the 'vicars', the minor clergy who either stood in for, or supplemented, the prebendaries of the minster. These 'vicars' had once lived dispersed through this relatively small town, but, after reports of a series of 'abuses', they were settled in purpose-built housing under Bishop Ralph of Shrewsbury. The vicars were accommodated in a double terrace of forty-two, two-roomed houses facing one another in a street closed at one end by a chapel and at the other by a common hall. The Vicars' Close looks rather like a contemporary

Oxford college. The hall and the Vicars' Close were connected to the cathedral by a gallery leading off the chapter house stairs and crossing the Chain Gate at first-floor level. Though none of the vicars' houses survives in anything like its original state, both the hall and the chapel survive pretty much intact (though both have been much restored). Beyond its extraordinary charm, what now gives the complex its distinction is the evidence it provides of the ordered, communal life of a great medieval religious establishment.

EXETER CATHEDRAL

Until the so-called 'Baedeker Raid' of 1942 – two nights of bombing which wrecked so much of the historic centre of Exeter – that cathedral city too boasted a college of vicars choral. At Exeter it was an infinitely more modest establishment than that at Wells, but pre-war photographs show a pleasingly panelled hall which survives now only as a sad and unloved ruin on the south-west corner of Cathedral Close. Although the cathedral itself lost one medieval chapel in the raid, it was otherwise mercifully spared. Its major medieval fittings had already been removed for safe-keeping but a good deal of Victorian glass was blown out (and in the 1940s few regretted its loss). The post-war restoration of the cathedral was generally highly conservative, but it did entail the removal of the important (and costly) marble and alabaster reredos, inlaid with semi-precious stones, that had been designed by Gilbert Scott in the 1870s. The reredos was, alas, exiled to an Exeter parish church. It should be brought back.

The Cathedral Close, or 'Green', at Exeter must always have given the impression of a semi-urban rather than an exclusively ecclesiastical space. If it once had gates, it lost them long ago, and the north side of the Green is taken up with a pleasingly varied range of commercial buildings, including the first inn in England to be re-designated by the more sophisticated name of an 'hotel' (now the Royal Clarence Hotel). At Exeter, city and church thus seem to interact more than they do in other southern cathedral cities. Surprisingly to some, until 1971 the western façade of the

Exeter Cathedral from the north-west, showing the Norman crossing towers.

cathedral was partly hidden by the Victorian parish church of St Mary Major, an unfortunate red sandstone structure that tended to glare at its august neighbour rather than nod respectfully to it. The church is not much missed but its site still renders the proportions of the Close somewhat awkward, especially so as its disappearance has exposed some deeply second-rate post-war structures to view. Exeter Cathedral lost its cloisters in the mid-seventeenth century (the city corporation opened a market on their site) and the fragmentary south-east corner of a cloister that now stands in their place is the result of a nineteenth-century restoration. The rectangular chapter house is handsome enough, but it could not hold its own in comparison to the glories of those at Salisbury, Lincoln and Wells. In the absence of a cloister walk the chapter house is generally entered from the south transept and in no sense does it seem to form an organic part of the cathedral's architecture. The important chapter library, which was once housed in the Lady Chapel, was moved here in the early nineteenth century. It was moved again after the Second World War. Having been emptied of its shelves, the chapter house has now been marred by some truly horrid fibreglass sculptures which have been placed in niches.

All this might serve to suggest that Exeter Cathedral is a poor relation to the other great secular cathedrals of England. Nothing could be further from the truth. When a visitor enters the church from its west end the impact of its richly glorious vault is breathtaking. Unlike French cathedrals, Exeter does not soar upwards to a high, narrow vault; unlike Lincoln or Wells, its luxurious vaulting system cannot be described as quirky or quizzical. However, Exeter expresses its glory immediately and fulfillingly. It stretches above one's head from west to east, in an unbroken, richly expressive line of ribs that open like palm-fronds The long line of Exeter's vault exists because, although the cathedral has transepts, there is no central tower and therefore no real 'crossing' to divide the roof spaces of the nave from those of the choir. When the minster was rebuilt in the Gothic style in the thirteenth and fourteenth centuries, its architects retained the two Norman towers which still serve as transepts. The arrangement is unique in England (though it was imitated in the nearby Devon church at Ottery St Mary, and can

The West Window of Exeter Cathedral showing the westernmost bays of the nave vault constructed in the late fourteenth century. The modern glass is a replacement for the window designed by G.F. Bodley, which was blown out in the air-raid of 1942.

occasionally be met with in German cathedrals). From the outside, the Norman towers seem ungainly, but their presence is forgotten once one enters an interior space of unsurpassed sophistication.

The parish churches of Devon are famed for their richly carved wooden rood screens. These screens, which divide naves from chancels, are now uniformly deprived of the 'rood' (that is, the cross bearing the crucified Christ) they once displayed, but even in their truncated form they still suggest the pride and prosperity of the parishes that erected them. The early fourteenth-century 'rood screen' in Exeter Cathedral is of stone rather than wood, and it too lacks its 'rood', but its splendour echoes that of the most elaborate screens in the diocese. The cathedral's screen is properly referred to as a 'pulpitum' and, if anything, it has a kinship with the great *jubés* in the larger churches in Belgium. It is probable that the Exeter pulpitum always provided a base for the cathedral's organ and that the rood proper stood on a metal beam above it. The screen consists of three handsome ogee (that is, an upright double curve) arched openings. The openings to the choir on either side of the central arch were only created in the 1870s, but they give the screen an added lightness. It was also argued by the Victorian restorers who created the openings that this was a return to the medieval scheme. That may well be so. The two opened arches now shelter altars as they certainly did in the fourteenth century. Above the three arches runs a further series of thirteen smaller ogee arches decorated with paintings of scriptural subjects. These clumsy paintings probably only date from the early seventeenth century, but were once covered in plaster and were only rediscovered when a workman's ladder, propped against one of them in 1870, cracked the offending plaster-work. The screen is surmounted by an organ case which dates from 1665 and which prominently bears the name of the organ-builder, John Loosemore, who had earlier been sent to Cornwall by the Restoration dean, Seth Ward, to select the best tin for the pipes.

The Exeter screen defines the generous proportions of the cathedral's choir, the chief glory of which is the towering wooden canopy of the Bishop's Throne. It dates from 1312 and appears to have originally been coloured white and gold but it now has the exquisite richness of well-oiled, ancient oak. This is a 'cathedra' *par excellence* and is unrivalled by the throne canopies of any other English bishop, for it reaches up nearly to the crest of the vault. The bishops of Exeter are enthroned in a tabernacle that resembles one of the great medieval sacrament houses of the continent. Gilbert Scott, the Victorian restorer of the cathedral, must have felt the influence of this canopy when he designed the Albert Memorial in Kensington Gardens in the mid-1860s. But the Bishop of Exeter's throne is no memorial. It is a living reminder both of what a bishop represents and, by extension, what a bishop's church truly is.

3

THE REFORMATION
CATHEDRALS

REFORMATION, DEFORMATION AND RE-CREATION

THE RELIGIOUS CHANGES WROUGHT by the Tudor kings and queens
in the sixteenth century changed England for ever. Those reforms
and counter-reforms not only altered the character of the rites and
ceremonies celebrated in English cathedrals, they transformed the
decoration and the fittings of every church in the land, both great and
small. The fact that the ancient cathedrals now proudly profess that
the daily worship they offer is part of an unbroken continuum often
disguises the truly radical nature of the Reformation in England.

An informed and sympathetic foreign visitor is likely to look on
the quality of worship in English cathedrals with envy. Surpliced
choirs sing matins and evensong on most days in the year and a
properly vested clergy perform their liturgical obligations on a
regular basis. Due dignity of worship is observed throughout and
that worship emphatically testifies to the fact that these cathedrals
are far from historical anomalies. The medieval cathedrals of
England embody the very best features of living Anglicanism: its
order, its sense of tradition, and its (generally) exemplary balance of
thanksgiving, prayer and music.

Nevertheless, a ghostly visitant from medieval England would
find these churches unrecognizable and their worship alien. This
would not be true if this same spectre were allowed to explore the

great Gothic cathedrals of Spain or Germany. English cathedrals have for the most part been stripped both of their vibrant colours and of the glory of their ancient imagery. Roods, altars and reredoses have been systematically dismantled, statues have been defaced, stained glass smashed and shrines desecrated and removed. At first sight such acts of desecration may no longer be obvious for, thanks to the energy of Victorian restorers and the discrimination of latter-day benefactors, much of the damage wrought in the sixteenth and seventeenth centuries has been repaired, replaced or covered up. What is noticeable in English cathedrals, however, is the absence of what one might call the accoutrements of medieval devotion. The great cathedrals were originally designed to house a complex system of ceremonies, rites and images. The elaborate tombs of bishops and noblemen survive, but the lavishly decorated altars endowed by those bishops and noblemen have been deprived of the images of saints and angels that once made them wonders. The over-arching architecture of the great cathedrals was once complemented by a wealth of decorative detail. Not only was imagery integral to the architectural scheme of a great church, but a whole series of saints' shrines, chantry chapels and dedicated altars reflected in miniature the greater structure that contained them. A great medieval church was conceived of not as a single space but as a series of interconnected and integrated spaces.

The radical changes to the interiors of English cathedrals came gradually. Under Henry VIII, whose doctrinal definitions tended to be conservative, the main attack was aimed at cathedral finances and at the rich shrines of those saints who were deemed to be 'politically incorrect'. The sequestrated wealth found its way into royal coffers. Particular venom was directed at the cult of St Thomas à Becket. His relics were displaced and his elaborate shrine at Canterbury was dismantled, its jewels being acquired by the royal treasury. His feast days were abolished and even Becket's name was scratched out of missals in order to eradicate the pious memory of an archbishop who had dared to oppose the will of his sovereign. The relics of other English saints, most of them churchmen by profession, fared similarly. As pilgrimages were now discouraged, the revenues from pious visitors dried up accordingly. Only St Cuthbert's bones were reverently reburied at Durham Cathedral, though the precious shrine that once contained them was broken up. At Westminster Abbey, however, the bones of St Edward the Confessor, the patron saint of the kings of England and the ancestor from whom those kings claimed the power to cure scrofula, the disease once known as 'the king's evil', were treated with unparalleled respect. Henry VIII's commissioners were challenging saints who rivalled the authority of kings, not the idea of a sainted king. Thus, St Edward still rests in a plain but handsome shrine constructed in the reign of Mary I and left undamaged by her successors.

In the short reign of Edward VI the liturgy of the Church was radically simplified and rendered into the English language. Certain religious images deemed to be 'superstitious' (notably the great roods, the images of the crucified Christ with Mary and John on each side) were removed and destroyed. The abolition of chantries meant a substantial diminution not only of the attached revenues, but also of the number of priests and chaplains once required to say the now redundant Masses for the dead. Queen Mary's determined attempt to revive the fortunes of Catholic England died with her in 1558, and under Elizabeth the English church fell steadily under the control of bishops and senior clergy resolved to advance the cause of a moderate, but decidedly anti-Papal, Protestantism. This entailed the wholesale disappearance of the ceremonial of the Catholic Mass and of the vestments and altar furnishings associated with it. Even processions were now forbidden, notably those integrally linked to the ceremonies of Candlemas, Maundy Thursday, Palm Sunday, and Good Friday. The great roods, which had loomed over cathedral naves, were again dismantled. The statues on the now semi-redundant choir-screens were defaced (unless they were, as at York Minster, representations of kings); images in precious metals were melted down; embroidered hangings, banners and altar frontals were sold or burned; wall-paintings were whitewashed and replaced with instructive scriptural quotations. The multiple stone altars were all broken, leaving but one, stark wooden communion table in the now unadorned cathedral chancels. It is sometimes argued that yet more damage to the fabric of the great English churches was perpetrated by bigoted Puritan iconoclasts in the first half of the seventeenth century, but it is undoubtedly true that it was the religious changes sponsored by the Tudors that did the greatest damage to the complex visual and ecclesiological heritage of the medieval centuries. It was irreplaceable.

Once the Tudor monarchs took upon themselves the exclusive right to appoint both bishops and senior cathedral clergy, those clergymen became active instruments of the State. It was they who physically reformed their cathedrals, often against the wishes of the old, more conservative, chapter members who assumed that they were still in control. At Exeter Cathedral, for example, the new dean appointed by Henry VIII and encouraged by the King's minister, Thomas Cromwell, personally took it upon himself to purge his church of 'superstition' and to 'reform' both its worship and the responsibilities of its chapter. This new dean, Simon Heynes, was armed with a passionate conviction and with royal authority, and the disgruntled canons found themselves powerless to oppose him.

It is scarcely surprising that many of the Catholic composer, William Byrd's, most beautiful Latin motets sing of a desolate Jerusalem and a ruined Temple. The implications would not have been lost on his English co-religionists. Just as the Pope had been displaced as the head of the English Church, so too were all the outward signs of 'Popish' religion. Radical English Protestants, egged on by royal authority, were determined to extirpate what were deemed to be the 'rags of popery'. These acts of purgation might well have been justified in the name of a 'reformed' religion, but they were not paralleled in Lutheran Germany. Most of the ancient cathedrals of northern Germany lost their status as cathedrals when they lost their bishops, but they still retained their great roods, their rood screens, their statues, their emptied but towering sacrament houses and their well-stocked treasuries. The great English churches were 'purified' while, outwardly at least, their German equivalents were time-locked in the 1540s. As lovers of Dutch paintings know, this was not the case in the neighbouring Calvinist Netherlands, where churches were stripped of their imagery and whitewashed clean of any Popish taint. Perhaps the nearest parallel to the devastation wrought in the interiors of English cathedrals in the sixteenth century is the fate of most of the greater French churches at the hands of Revolutionaries in the

1790s. Tombs of kings, bishops and noblemen were ransacked and all traces of 'feudal' heraldry erased. Even though their religious motives were radically different, English Puritans and French Jacobins shared an ingrained ideological hatred of the Catholic Church and its ministers and a cultivated distaste for the trappings of Catholicism. In both instances a new age was deemed to have dawned and cathedrals were obliged to find a new function.

CHANGES WITHIN THE CATHEDRAL CLOSE

Under Edward VI a major social change complemented the ritual and theological novelties of the Reformation. A married clergy gradually became the norm after 1549, changing the character of cathedral closes for ever. The precedent had been set by Henry VIII's acquiescent Archbishop of Canterbury, Thomas Cranmer. King Henry was probably not personally acquainted with Mrs Cranmer, whom the Archbishop had married secretly in Germany. In England Mrs Cranmer was kept discreetly and generally unacknowledged in the shadows. Exactly what the status of the wives of the upper clergy was seems to have remained a contentious question until the end of the sixteenth century. A bishop's spouse had none of the social standing of the wife of a secular peer of the realm and was accorded none of the honour. Despite actively promoting married clergy, Elizabeth's uncertainty as to how she should address the wife of Archbishop Matthew Parker is suggested by the Queen's famous put-down to her hostess. Having been richly entertained at Lambeth Palace Elizabeth offered thanks for Margaret Parker's 'good cheer' by first insisting that she could not call her 'madam' for that would have accorded her too high a status. Elizabeth made her disquiet even more evident when she admitted that nor could she address Mrs Parker as 'mistress' (for that would imply that she was no better than a merchant's wife). Nevertheless, Elizabeth's thanks were taken graciously. One is led to wonder, however, quite how easily the new wives and children of provincial bishops, deans and canons were accepted into the society of cathedral closes, which until recently had been the exclusive preserve of a celibate male clergy.

MONASTIC BUILDINGS DURING THE DISSOLUTION

The fundamental change to the constitution of ancient monastic cathedrals was the inexorable pace of the dissolution of the religious houses attached to them. There was nothing new about closing smaller or semi-redundant monasteries in order to redeploy their financial and architectural assets. Jesus College at Cambridge had been founded by Bishop Alcock of Ely in 1497. In order to do so, Alcock suppressed a Benedictine nunnery (which had latterly housed only two nuns) and used the convent as his college. Similarly, in 1525 Cardinal Wolsey's far more ambitious 'Cardinal College' at Oxford (now Christ Church) took over the site of the suppressed priory of St Frideswide. Wolsey planned an extravagant rebuild of the monastic church, but his fall put a stop to his grand scheme. As a consequence, the truncated priory church first became the college chapel and was then called upon to double-up as the cathedral of the newly created diocese of Oxford.

In the late 1530s the state of affairs had changed radically. Now Henry himself demanded the surrender of the land, assets and even the buildings, of every monastic house in England. There was no declared intention of reusing their resources for charitable or educational purposes. This was a battle of State against Church, and the State, having rejected the superior authority of Rome, was determined to achieve ecclesiastical submission. Thanks to the efficiency of the rapacious King's minister, Thomas Cromwell, and his commissioners, the greater monasteries, including those that were anciently at the heart of cathedral establishments, disappeared between 1539 and 1540. The Abbey at Ely was surrendered in 1539 and its Benedictine monks pensioned off. In the following year Worcester and Rochester Cathedrals lost their priories and Canterbury and Durham their large Benedictine houses. At both Canterbury and Durham the administration of the cathedral was handed over to a dean and twelve canons. They, and other former monastic cathedrals, now became cathedrals of what were called the 'new foundation'. At Durham twelve former monks were appointed to prebends (or residential canonries) and the last prior, Hugh Whitehead, became the cathedral's first dean in 1541, comfortably living in the very commodious old mansion that still serves his successors as a deanery.

As we have seen, many of the monastery buildings at Durham survive. The former refectory was converted into a library in the seventeenth century and the substantial monks' dormitory took on a similar function in the nineteenth. The chapter house suffered severe damage in the late eighteenth century, but was ably restored a hundred years later. At Canterbury, by contrast, relatively little of the old monastery is left standing. The cloister and chapter house are fine but the monks' infirmary is a melancholy ruin and most of the other survivals (such as the deanery, the former Prior's Lodging) have been considerably reconstructed over the centuries. Worcester Cathedral only retains its cloister and chapter house and Rochester, having lost even its cloister, can only boast of desultory fragments of its ancient priory. At Ely all that now remains of the great monastery is incorporated into the King's School. The precincts of Winchester Cathedral, however, have virtually nothing to remind us of its ancient Benedictine community.

Visitors to the historic cities of Canterbury, York and Winchester might easily be forgiven for not seeking out the remains of the three great monastic houses that once added to the religious and cultural life of those cathedral cities. These were great monasteries distinct from the religious houses attached to their respective cathedrals. None of these remains are now particularly impressive, certainly when compared to the spectacular ruins of Fountains or Rievaulx Abbey. The stones of the abandoned St Augustine's Abbey at Canterbury, of St Mary's at York and of Hyde Abbey at Winchester were quarried for other, generally secular, structures in the centuries after the Dissolution. At Winchester barely a trace now exists of the venerable Hyde Abbey, the resting place of King Alfred the Great, his wife and his immediate successors. At Canterbury the only substantial survival of the even more venerable St Augustine's Abbey is the gateway, though, beyond this free-standing gate, the precinct of the lost abbey now boasts a fine college building by William Butterfield dating from the 1840s. The desecrated tombs of Augustine and other sainted early archbishops of Canterbury are now, thanks to archaeological endeavour, just about discernible. At York the fragment of what must have been the hugely impressive, and once very wealthy,

St Mary's Abbey now stands like an immense garden ornament in the finely laid-out grounds of the Yorkshire Museum.

The most dramatic loss amongst the monastic cathedrals was the large abbey of St Mary at Coventry. The church had been raised to cathedral rank in 1095. The sixteenth-century bishop of what had become the diocese of Coventry and Lichfield was not completely bereft of a cathedral for he retained his great church at Lichfield. Nevertheless, the city of Coventry lost what appears to have been a major Romanesque church, and its demolition was so thorough that only parts of the foundations are now visible (and these were uncovered by archaeologists following the destructive bombing of the city during the Second World War). The fuller story of Coventry's vicissitudes as a cathedral city can be read in Chapter 6.

The Dissolution of the English abbeys and the sequestration of their property meant not only a radical shift in the nature of land ownership, but also in the constitution of the realm. The greater abbots, who had included those of St Albans, St Augustine's Canterbury, St Mary's York, Westminster, Glastonbury and Bury St Edmund's, had been granted the privilege not only of episcopal status, but also the right of a seat in the House of Lords. The loss of these 'mitred abbots' therefore reduced the influence of the Church in Parliament. This, coupled with the abolition of Papal jurisdiction and the right of Rome to appoint bishops, gave the Crown effective control of virtually every aspect of the English Church. The one surviving 'mitred abbot' is, incongruously enough, the Bishop of Norwich, for when Henry VIII confiscated the revenues of the diocese, he substituted them with those formerly attached to the abbeys of St Benet and Hickling. Norwich Cathedral may have lost its own abbey when it was refounded in 1538, but its bishop technically remains abbot of the now utterly ruinous St Benet's at Horning (the only English abbey, incidentally, to have escaped dissolution, if not ultimate desolation).

THE HENRICIAN BISHOPRICS

Henry VIII used his new position as the self-appointed Supreme Head of the Church of England to establish a series of new dioceses.

The six new bishops, selected by the king, took the places in the House of Lords of the now defunct mitred abbots. A small portion of the sequestered monastic resources was transferred to the new bishops and six redundant abbey churches became their cathedrals. It tells us a good deal about the demographics of Tudor England that five of the six new dioceses were situated in the southern province of Canterbury (only Chester is in the Province of York). Westminster Abbey was reconstituted as a cathedral in 1540 with its bishop's diocese stretching over the county of Middlesex. The see of Gloucester was created in September 1541 with St Peter's Abbey as its bishop's church. The same year saw the elevations of St Peter's Abbey at Peterborough, of Oseney Abbey (to the west of Oxford), and of St Werburgh's Abbey at Chester as the respective cathedrals of the new dioceses of Peterborough, Oxford and Chester. At Bristol in June 1542 the redundant St Augustine's Abbey became the cathedral of an oddly-shaped small diocese containing the city, its immediate hinterland and the detached county of Dorset. The Letters Patent that established the new see spoke of the hope of establishing 'true religion and true worship of God' in the place of 'the enormities into which the life and profession of monks in the long course of time had most deplorably fallen'. The first bishop of Bristol, Paul Bush, a former (and now married) monk was to be assisted by a dean and six canons, but his cathedral was in a poor state of repair. Its nave had been demolished by the monks in preparation for the construction of a new one, and now a lack of both funds and will precluded any continuation of this ambitious work. As a consequence, the church remained a truncated stump until a fitting nave was added in the late 1860s.

CHRIST CHURCH CATHEDRAL, OXFORD

These six new dioceses were reduced to five when Mary I suppressed the see of Westminster in 1556 and the abbey was returned to its ancient purpose as a Benedictine house. When this brief monastic restoration ended on the accession of Elizabeth in 1558 Westminster Abbey became what it is now: a so-called Royal Peculiar, a church administered by a dean and chapter under the direct authority of the sovereign. The diocese of Oxford survived and flourished, but rapidly found itself without a cathedral when Oseney Abbey, an Augustinian foundation, was purloined by Henry VIII and demolished. Barely a trace of the abbey is visible now for its ruins served as a useful source of building stone when Charles I fortified Oxford against his Parliamentary enemies in the 1640s. The first bishop of Oxford, the former Abbot of Oseney, Robert King, was reduced to accepting the old priory church of St Frideswide as his cathedral in 1546. Oxford was, and is, unique amongst English cathedrals in that it is embedded in a university college, Christ Church, Cardinal Wolsey's college refounded by Henry VIII. It is the smallest of the English cathedrals, having lost half of its nave when Wolsey laid out what he intended to be a splendid court for his college (now Tom Quad). Wolsey's architects managed to build a magnificent college hall and a kitchen to the south of this court, but the proposed, vast, vaulted cloister-like quad was never completed. Nor was the new college chapel. This chapel might well have rivalled that of another royal foundation, King's College at Cambridge. When Wolsey fell from grace in 1529 funds immediately dried up and Henry was evidently not minded to replace them either for the benefit of his new bishop or his new college. Having served as an awkwardly shaped chapel for thirteen years, the old church of St Frideswide was designated an even more awkwardly shaped cathedral. The new foundation was served by a dean and six canons, who also formed part of the governing body of the college. The truncated proportions of Oxford Cathedral do not necessarily diminish its elegance, but much of its attraction lies in the quality of its fittings rather than in its structural pretension. Uniquely amongst English cathedrals, little of it is visible, hemmed in as it is by its college. Apart from the distant prospect of its tower and spire, the only good view of it is obtained from one of the private college gardens. It only just holds its own amidst the architectural wonders of the university city that surrounds it. It would be a very different story had Oseney 'Cathedral' survived Henry's rapacity.

Bristol Cathedral

Thanks to the grand scale of the, albeit unfinished, Tom Quad, there was never any real possibility of reconstructing the missing bays of the nave of Christ Church Cathedral. The same was not true of the foreshortened Bristol Cathedral. That cathedral had not fared well in the first half of the nineteenth century. In 1831 the city of Bristol had suffered severely from riots, directed in part against Bishop Robert Gray who had opposed the Reform Bill in the House of Lords. During these riots the adjacent bishop's palace and library were destroyed by fire and the cathedral itself came under threat of destruction. The bishopric of Bristol was joined to that of Gloucester in 1836 and was only restored as a distinct see in 1897. Where the monastic nave had once stood, dwelling houses had been constructed. When these houses were demolished in 1835 (by a dean and chapter fearful of further incendiarism), the former central tower was left exposed with its base serving as a clumsy west end of the church. It gradually became evident that this tower had become structurally unsound and was in need of underpinning. Its battlements and pinnacles were removed for safety reasons and the cathedral was left as an embarrassing eyesore, prominently sited in the very centre of what had become a prosperous and burgeoning Victorian port city. Things were made worse when improvements to the layout of neighbouring streets exposed the foundations of the nave, work on which had been abandoned in 1526. This discovery prompted action and in 1868 the architect George Edmund Street was called upon to design a new nave in a style approximating to the superbly inventive fourteenth-century work to its east. The new nave was also intended to complement the daring lierne vault in the crossing area (completed in 1480). Street also added the two western towers between 1884–8. A further restoration in the years 1890–1904 entailed a re-ordering of the interior. This work, directed by J.L. Pearson and his son, gave the cathedral a new reredos and a choir screen with wide, open ogee arches. Thus, when the bishopric was restored at the end of the century, it could at least boast a handsome cathedral. Bristol Cathedral happily marries sensitive modern work to the ravishingly daring architecture of its serene fourteenth-century choir, its exquisitely vaulted aisles and the handsome Lady Chapel. Street and the Pearsons were well aware that their work at Bristol was conventional enough, especially so when compared to the wayward genius of the medieval architects, but it represented an assertion of the continuity of the Gothic as a living style into the late nineteenth century.

GLOUCESTER CATHEDRAL

The choir of Gloucester Cathedral looking westwards with the Norman nave beyond.

The great medieval abbey at Gloucester was founded by King Osric of Mercia in the seventh century and dedicated to St Peter. Its status had been further advanced in the 1380s when its abbot was granted the privilege of a mitre. Both the monastery and the city had retained their strong royal connections and could always claim a far more elevated status than mercantile Bristol. The abbey buildings, rebuilt in the 1050s, provided agreeable and commodious

89

enough accommodation for both William the Conqueror and William Rufus to elect to spend a series of sumptuous Christmases here. It is claimed that the Conqueror ordered the production of the Domesday Book in council in the abbey's chapter house. His eldest son, Robert Curthose, Duke of Normandy, is buried under a fine wooden monument in the south ambulatory. Most medieval kings continued to pay extensive visits to the abbey, and the title 'Duke of Gloucester', first created in 1385, has remained linked to the sons of monarchs. The 9-year-old Henry III was hurriedly crowned in the abbey church following the defeat of his unruly barons, but pre-Reformation Gloucester's greatest claim to national fame was the much-visited tomb of Edward II. The king had been ceremonially interred here in 1327 following his murder at Berkeley Castle (the body had been publicly exposed in an attempt to prove, somewhat implausibly, that no foul play had been involved in his death). It is said the Bristol Abbey had tactfully refused to take responsibility for the corpse, but Gloucester's honourable charity was to prove both politic and profitable in the long run.

Given these substantial royal connections it is not surprising to find that the Act of Parliament that created the see of Gloucester after the suppression of the Benedictine abbey noted that 'the late monastery in which the monument of our renowned ancestor the King of England is erected, is a very fit and proper place....' It is evident from this statement that royal history had taken precedence over architecture in the promotion of Gloucester Abbey to the rank of a cathedral. That being said, Gloucester Cathedral is one of the most gorgeously awe-inspiring religious buildings in the land. The survival of the great church after the suppression of the abbey is therefore singularly happy. If very little now remains either of the monastery buildings or of the medieval city of Gloucester, the fabric of the cathedral possesses an extraordinary and redemptory *presence* within an often unlovely city. From certain angles the exterior of the church might seem ungainly, but that ungainliness is relieved by the soaring majesty of its central tower. The great Perpendicular choir, grandly rebuilt in the late fourteenth century for the communal worship of the Benedictine monks, is noticeably higher than the Romanesque nave to the west of the tower. It is only on entering

The choir of Gloucester
Cathedral showing the
East Window and the vault
begun c.1337.

Gloucester Cathedral that we become aware that virtually every architectural element in the nave of the church is but a prelude to its greatest glory: the stupendous choir.

The transformation of the eastern arm of the church is one of the great triumphs of the new Perpendicular style – a style that emerged late in the reign of Edward III and began to mature in that of Richard II. Royal architects and royal patronage are in evidence at Gloucester, possibly as an act of homage to the late Edward II (whose state funeral was held in December 1327 in the presence of Edward's widow and his young heir, Edward III). It is known that valuable royal 'oblations', presented at the tomb, were redeemed for funds that contributed to the wholesale reconstruction of the choir area. The sturdy regularity of Gloucester's gloomy Norman nave is handsome enough, but beyond the choir screen the mood changes utterly. Here the heavy Norman work has been transformed into a single, soaring light-filled space, with a complex lierne vault held aloft by slender, vertical stone pinnacles. The insistent verticality is relieved by delicate tracery and by what can best be described as stone 'panelling' that masks the surviving Romanesque arches and the shaved columns. The greatest triumph is perhaps the huge east window, finished in the mid-fourteenth century and still filled with its original glass, including the coats of arms of noblemen who fought in the battle of Crécy. The sides of the window are slightly bowed, an effect that adds to the extraordinarily animated feel of whole design. The Lady Chapel that lies beyond this great window was finished at the beginning of the sixteenth century but retains the stylistic daring, the light and the consistency of the earlier choir. It is partly detached from the choir, permitting the filtered light to glow through the great east window without interference from behind. The effect of these two vast single-cell spaces must have astounded contemporaries. The same could be said of the confident exploitation of the new system of fan vaulting in Gloucester's cloisters (built 1351–1377). Some Victorian purists, such as John Ruskin, distrusted the Perpendicular style, and especially its last and greatest triumph, the fan-vaulted chapel of King's College Chapel at Cambridge. The starry, lierne-vaulted choir at Gloucester is effectively the crucial precursor to King's Chapel, where the fan vaulting system, pioneered at Gloucester, reached perfection. King's Chapel may be deemed the final triumph of the perpendicular style, but the structural daring of Gloucester's choir and Lady Chapel quite outclasses any rival.

Gloucester Cathedral from the north-east engraved by J. Le Keux from the drawing by W.H. Bartlett which was published in Britton's *The History and Antiquities of the Abbey and Cathedral Church of Gloucester* (1829).

Peterborough Cathedral

The royal connections of the abbey at Peterborough were less exalted and less historically rooted than those of Gloucester, but they probably weighed heavily on the consciousness (and perhaps even the conscience) of Henry VIII. Here, in 1536, were interred the remains of Henry's rejected wife, Catherine of Aragon. Henry had acrimoniously divorced her and attempted to enforce acceptance of his second wife, Anne Boleyn, but many of his subjects retained a fierce loyalty to Catherine and the King, frustrated as he was, somehow maintained a respect for Catherine's abiding dignity in her lonely final years. Catherine's burial at Peterborough may well have saved the great minster from an alienation and degradation akin to hers. Henry founded a new diocese here in September 1541, carving it out of the huge medieval see of Lincoln. Peterborough Cathedral is, however, sited on the very edge of the diocese of Ely (whose borders begin half a mile away on the other side of the River Nene). The last Abbot of Peterborough, John Chambers, became its first bishop, and four of his former monks, canons of the new cathedral. Henry allocated a third of the abbey's income to the new bishop, and a further third to the chapter, but, typically enough, he kept the remaining third of its resources for the royal coffers.

Peterborough Abbey had been founded in 655 on a strip of land that rises above the fertile, surrounding Fenland. This once-remote settlement was known to the Anglo-Saxons as Medeshamstede ('the homestead in the meadows'), but such was the local power of this abbey dedicated to St Peter that a new name was gradually adopted by the monastery and the small settlement surrounding it. The abbots of what became an immensely rich monastic community also had jurisdiction over the detached administrative area called 'the Soke of Peterborough'. Until the mid-nineteenth century Peterborough remained a small market town dominated by its great church, rather like nearby Ely. It was some miles east from the Great North Road and in 1801 it had a population of only some four thousand souls.

Perhaps because it was considered to be usefully out of the way, the new cathedral church was belatedly selected as a dig-nified resting place for the remains of a second Catholic queen,

Mary Queen of Scots. Mary was beheaded in February 1587 at Fotheringhay Castle, which lay in the new diocese. It was, however, eighteen months after her execution that Mary's body was brought to the cathedral for burial. The funeral procession took place by night, accompanied by torches, and the body was interred in the nave aisle opposite the tomb of Catherine of Aragon. There was no requiem Mass, but the following day the safely Protestant Bishop of Lincoln preached a funeral sermon. The ceremonies, such as befitted a queen, were performed according to the new Anglican rite. Twenty-five years later Mary's son, James VI of Scotland and I of England, moved her remains to Westminster Abbey, where she was re-interred in a fine tomb in the aisle of Henry VII's Chapel, parallel to that which contains the monument of her nemesis, Elizabeth I.

The city of Peterborough changed radically when the railway arrived in 1843. Its population had risen to 15,000 by 1871 and in 1874 it was granted a charter of incorporation (it had been up to that time the only city in England without a mayor and corporation). The railway town, served in the nineteenth century by five separate companies, expanded rapidly again during the last quarter of the twentieth century. The character of the city has now changed again from that of a relative backwater to a commercial hub, but the great minster on its low hill still holds its own. With York and Durham cathedrals, it remains one of the sights that impress and divert alert rail travellers on the East Coast Line.

Despite its former remoteness, Peterborough Cathedral has proved particularly susceptible to acts of wilful destruction. The Saxon minster was plundered by Hereward the Wake, as part of his Fenland campaign against the Conqueror. What remained of the pre-Norman church was wrecked by a devastating fire in 1116. It was in turn replaced by the great, stark Romanesque building that has largely survived to modern times. The exquisite fan-vaulted 'New Building' (as it is still known) was added as an eastern ambulatory in 1496–1508 and may well be the work of John Wastell before he designed the great fan vault at King's College at Cambridge. The old Lady Chapel was situated, as at Ely, to the east of the north transept, but fell victim to the ruthless iconoclasts who did vast damage to the fabric of the cathedral during the Civil War

The fan vault of the 'New Building' at Peterborough Cathedral was perhaps designed by John Wastell and constructed 1496–1508.

period. Apart from the demolition of the Lady Chapel, Cromwellian soldiers smashed all the cathedral's stained glass and destroyed the abbey cloisters, the church's two organs, its reredos and its choir stalls. Many of the tombs (including that of Catherine of Aragon) were mutilated. The present dignity of the interior of Peterborough Cathedral owes much to the Victorian architect, J.L. Pearson, who reconstructed the crossing and its tower and re-ordered the choir, giving it a handsome mosaic pavement and, above all, in 1894, a new, glorious free-standing marble and alabaster 'ciborium' which shelters the high altar.

CHESTER CATHEDRAL

The thorough Victorian restoration at Peterborough Cathedral not only preserved its structure, it also undid much of the damage inflicted on the building during the seventeenth century. The fifth of the Henrician cathedrals, Chester, underwent three even more rigorous nineteenth-century 'restorations' in 1844, 1868–76 and 1882. These 'restorations' have left it sometimes difficult to 'read' as a medieval structure. Chester had briefly been a Norman see, but this was suppressed in 1095. When Henry VIII reconstituted the diocese of Chester in 1541 he carved it out of the western part of the see of York and the northern part of Lichfield. The new diocese was for a long period the largest in England, stretching from Yorkshire to the borders of Cumberland. The cathedral church was the old Benedictine abbey of St Werburgh, and it still contains a particularly fine set of spiky late-fourteenth-century choir stalls which have served its secular clergy as splendidly as they had formerly served its monks. Appropriately, too, its last abbot was appointed as its first dean (its first bishop, John Bird, was a former provincial of the English Carmelites but was deprived in 1554 on account of his being married).

Though Chester is an ancient city, proud of its Roman origins, and a thriving medieval port and garrison, it is now substantially a Victorian construct of black-and-white buildings that persuade many visitors that its assumed air of antiquity is genuine. Its distinctive architectural character, imitative and adaptive of seventeenth-century half-timbering, is sometimes described as the 'Chester' style. In some important ways, therefore, this extensively renewed sandstone church, which sits so happily in the very middle of busy streets, is a fitting reflection of its city.

ENGLISH CATHEDRALS DURING THE CIVIL WAR AND COMMONWEALTH

Much of the beauty of the smaller and middle-sized cathedral cities lies in the fact that their great minsters seem, like Chester's, so integral to the urban landscape. Church spaces and commercial and domestic spaces interrelate in a happy marriage. As we have seen in the case of Peterborough Cathedral, however, the breakdown of the relationship between a bishop's church and civil society could prove architecturally perilous. This is particularly true of the Civil War period in the 1640s and 1650s. The damage done by Cromwell's troops at Peterborough can be paralleled elsewhere in England and popular cathedral histories frequently recount stories of wanton iconoclasm and purposeful sacrilege. Because of their size great churches conveniently served as improvised barracks for troops on the move and as stables for cavalry horses. It was not only convenience that dictated such acts of desecration. The English Civil War was to a great extent a struggle between religious conservatives and those men and women who earnestly sought a radical extension of the leading principles of the Reformation.

When Parliament triumphed over Charles I, episcopacy was abolished and bishops' churches not only lost their 'cathedral status', but also most of their income. In 1646 a Parliamentary ordinance decreed that all bishops' estates should be sold. Those of deans and chapters were similarly disposed of three years later. Anglican worship, as set out in the Book of Common Prayer, was prohibited. In the most drastic cases the great churches were simply stripped out and abandoned as had happened in Reformation Scotland. In the 1640s Carlisle Cathedral was described as 'like a great wild country church neither beautify'd nor adorn'd one whit

… The Communion … was administered and receiv'd in a wild and unreverent manner.' Shortly afterwards Carlisle's Norman nave was pulled down, leaving only its eastern parts to serve the few 'unreverent' worshippers. At Durham, Scottish soldiers held prisoner in the cathedral were moved to burn virtually all of its ancient woodwork in order to keep warm. At Canterbury Cathedral soldiers 'threw the altar over and over down the three altar steps, and left it lying with the heels upwards'. A further military visitation at Canterbury, led by a man nicknamed 'Blue Dick', resulted in the demolition of a newly erected font and in an assault on 'the inscriptions, figures and coats of arms engraven upon brass' which were 'torn off from the ancient monuments, and whatsoever there was of beauty or decency in the holy place was despoiled'. At Winchester the survival of the chantry of William of Wykeham is said to be due to Colonel Fiennes, an old boy of Wykeham's school. Nevertheless, enough brass was looted from monuments to have 'built a house as strong as the brazen towers of old romances'. In 1643 at Norwich a fanatical mob broke into the cathedral and destroyed stained glass, sculpture and the organ. 'The cathedral was filled with musketeers,' wrote one commentator, 'drinking and tobacconing [sic] as if it had turned alehouse.' At Exeter the cathedral organ pipes were melted down in the cloisters and tombs were rifled. It was even claimed that a 'most puritanical and beastly' mob had made the church 'a common jakes [lavatory] for the exonerations [sic] of nature, sparing no place, neither the altar not the pulpit'. In 1648 the desecrated cathedral at Exeter was taken over by two rival Protestant congregations, each of which aspired to worship at the same hours. The dispute over which congregation took precedence was temporarily resolved when a brick wall was built across the quire aisles and the screen, thus dividing the church into 'East Peter's' (given over to the Presbyterians) and 'Peter's West' (the former nave now a conventicle of the Independents). In Exeter the bishop's palace was bought from Parliament by the city and leased to a sugar-baker. Similarly, the Bishop of Durham's castle in his cathedral city was sold to the Lord Mayor of London who, given its distance from the capital, barely occupied it and allowed it to become severely dilapidated.

Perhaps no English cathedral suffered as severely during the Civil

War and Commonwealth as did Lichfield. Early in 1643 the city of Lichfield was garrisoned by Royalist troops, with the cathedral and its close forming an important part of the defences. The city was first attacked (ironically on the feast of the patron of the cathedral, St Chad) and fell after a three-day siege. It was re-taken for the King later in the year, but it again fell to the Parliamentarians in 1646, this time after a four-month siege. It was later reported that 'two thousand shot of great ordnance and fifteen hundred grenadoes had been discharged against the great church'. The west window was wrecked, the nave vaults destroyed and the central spire collapsed into the choir demolishing much of it. The victorious Parliamentary troops then went on the rampage, directing much of their fury at what survived of the stained glass and at the tombs of the medieval bishops. They were even said to have hunted a cat with hounds in the church and to have sacrilegiously baptized a calf at the font! One commentator, the historian Browne Willis, mourned that in 1646 'the Church had been so totally demolish'd ... that it may be truly said that there is not now remaining the least piece of Brass, Glass, Iron, Arms etc.' When Anglican services resumed at the time of the Restoration in June 1660, they had to be said in the chapter house – this being 'the only place in the church that had a roof to shelter them'.

The central spire, which with the two western spires gives the cathedral its particularly distinctive profile, was only reconstituted after a huge and expensive process of restoration in the years 1661–9. This vigorous campaign of reconstruction was directed by the determined new Bishop of Lichfield, John Hacket. Charles II gave a hundred oak trees, and his brother James, Duke of York, paid for a restoration of the destroyed West Window. The supposedly 'incorrect' tracery in this window and a statue of the king, which once stood in a niche above it, were removed in the nineteenth century (though the royal effigy is preserved in the cathedral). The church was re-dedicated, with great ceremony, on Christmas Eve 1669. Hacket's bold and extensive repairs endured unchanged for over a century, but in 1788 the dean and chapter called in the fashionable architect, James Wyatt, to conduct what was described as 'a thorough and substantial repair'. The canons had complained of cold draughts, so, with a remit to combat such discomforts, Wyatt

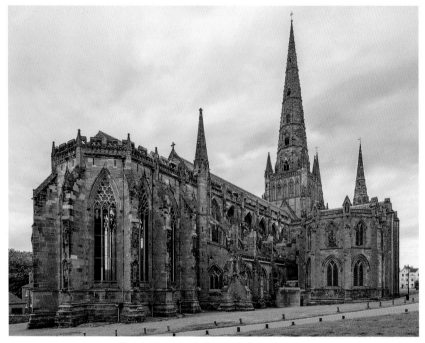

Lichfield Cathedral from the north-east.

set to work on a drastic re-ordering of the cathedral which parallels his intrusive work at Salisbury. He moved the altar eastwards
into the former Lady Chapel, walled up the arches in the aisles, and
erected a huge traceried glass screen to separate the nave from what
was now a narrow and artificially elongated choir. Apparently, the
canons still found their church cold! Nevertheless, when the anti-
quary, John Britton, visited and surveyed the cathedral in 1820, he
proclaimed its interior notable for its 'cleanness, cheerfulness and
elegance'. Such qualities, he implied, might well be happily imitated
in other less well-tended cathedrals.

The necessary intrusions of Bishop Hacket's craftsmen and the
gratuitous architectural innovations of James Wyatt were not to
the taste of more purist Victorian restorers. Consequently, they
were systematically undone. The pre-Victorian addition to Lichfield
Cathedral that happily survives is the fine set of early sixteenth-
century stained-glass windows which fill the (now restored) Lady
Chapel windows. This glass was rescued by a local landowner from

the dissolved abbey of Herckenrode in the Low Countries in 1802 and sold to Lichfield's dean and chapter. Herckenrode Abbey had fallen victim to the ruthless secularizations brought about by the advance of French Revolutionary troops. The anti-clerical French authorities at least had the grace – or the acumen – to sell the antique glass rather than shatter it. These old windows offer a worthy recompense for the terrible losses experienced by Lichfield Cathedral in the seventeenth century.

Much of what a modern visitor admires in the interior of Lichfield Cathedral is a product of the middle and later years of the nineteenth century. Sydney Smirke began this process of restoration in 1842–6. George Gilbert Scott continued it from 1857, and the work was finally completed by Scott's son, John Oldrid, in 1908. So thorough were these 'restorations' that it is often hard to determine what is medieval and what is a speculative replacement. Virtually all of the tracery in the cathedral's windows has been assiduously re-invented, as have most of the statues and decorative details of the western façade. Gilbert Scott removed Wyatt's glass screen and the arcades in the choir and moved the altar back to its original position (giving it an elaborate reredos in 1864). The new fittings in the choir, including the inlaid pavement, stalls and the bishop's throne,

The choir of Lichfield Cathedral. Much of the decorative detail shown, including the sculpture, choir stalls and the floor tiles, date from the Victorian restoration.

are impressive, but quite the handsomest of Scott's 'improvements' are the open-work iron, brass and copper screen of 1859–63 made by Francis Skidmore of Coventry and the elaborate iron pulpit in the nave (probably also by Skidmore). What the Victorian restorers found at Lichfield was an historic building profoundly damaged by war, iconoclasm, mindless vandalism and misguided tampering. What they left was an historic building transformed by the best that the nineteenth century could offer. As Richard John King declared in his guide to the English cathedrals, published in 1874, this was a restoration 'in the true sense'. Nothing, he asserted had been done 'for which there was not full authority'. We might well quibble at this claim but we cannot nowadays justifiably dispute King's assertion that the cathedral at Lichfield had been 'enriched with a series of works in wood, metal and encaustic tiles, unexceeded in beauty or in interest by any which have been produced in England during the present century'.

The century and a half of Reformation and Revolution that so dramatically changed England in the sixteenth and seventeenth centuries left all of its cathedrals bereft and some of them barely standing. The Restoration of the monarchy in 1660 brought with it a restoration of the Church of England. All of the old dioceses, both ancient and Henrician, were restored and the bishops returned to their own. The late Stuart period and the Georgian era that followed were, to an important degree, a time of consolidation both in Church and State. No new sees were established and, with the notable exception of St Paul's, no new cathedrals were built. Generally, the greater English churches appear to have been kept in good order. Once the damage inflicted in Cromwellian times had been repaired – or at least disguised – the now unadorned interiors of the medieval cathedrals became once again the setting for a regular pattern of Anglican liturgical worship. Bishops, deans and chapters replaced lost fittings with new ones in order to give their worship a proper dignity. Inevitably, however, changes in architectural fashion dictated that these fittings conformed to new styles.

They were therefore likely to strike later generations as incongruous, ugly and ultimately inappropriate and relatively few examples have survived nineteenth-century schemes of 'restoration'. The English Reformation meant that the English Church developed for some two centuries separately from much of the European mainstream, both Catholic and Protestant. The great medieval cathedrals inherited by the Church of England had been obliged to adjust to new patterns of worship in the sixteenth century. Thereafter, a succession of bishops, deans and chapters with responsibility for those cathedrals had to work out new ways of understanding the rich complexity of their architectural inheritance and, moreover, how to keep that inheritance in good order.

4

FROM ST PAUL'S CATHEDRAL TO BARCHESTER

ST PAUL'S CATHEDRAL, LONDON

The Original St Paul's

Inlaid in the floor of the nave of St Peter's Basilica in Rome, and frequently unnoticed by pilgrims because they are often covered by chairs, are the respective lengths of the greater Christian churches of the world. They include cathedrals from the New World as much as from the Old and they still suggest, as has always been intended, the huge and incomparable dimensions of St Peter's. St Peter's itself is not a cathedral (that distinction belongs to the Roman basilica of St John Lateran), but most of the other churches named are. It is quite a shock, therefore, to find St Paul's in London described in Latin not as *ecclesia cathedralis* ('cathedral church') but as *Fanum Sancti Pauli Londiniensis* ('the temple of St Paul in London'). When these names were inlaid in the floor in the pre-ecumenical days of the first half of the twentieth century, Catholics would properly have held that the modern St Paul's was indeed no 'cathedral'. Its medieval predecessor had been properly consecrated as the seat of a bishop approved by the Pope, but that cathedral had been destroyed in 1666. As the Church of Rome does not recognize the validity of Anglican orders, the Bishop of London is technically a layman and his 'cathedral' would once have been seen as a church consecrated according to rites regarded as void by the Bishop of Rome.

This slight to St Paul's Cathedral would not have been taken as such by the builders of the new cathedral or by the worthy succession of bishops of London since the reign of Charles II. For many of them, London's cathedral was the greatest church in the Protestant tradition, built as a proud rival to Roman pretensions and a declaration of faith in the dignity of the Church of England. One major nineteenth-century architectural critic, James Fergusson, declared St Paul's 'the largest and finest Protestant cathedral in the world, and, after, St Peter's, the most splendid church created in Europe since the revival of Classical Architecture.' Sir Christopher Wren's cathedral was more modest in scale than its lost predecessor, and could still be fitted inside St Peter's, but what it represented was unrivalled outside the Catholic world. Henry Hart Milman, the mid-Victorian Dean of St Paul's, was inordinately proud of the building in his charge and avidly defended what made it distinctive in comparison to St Peter's. The Roman basilica had been rebuilt with funds derived in part from the international sale of Indulgences, a practice that had provoked the fury of Martin Luther and sparked the Reformation in Germany:

> To rival St Peter's, to approach its unapproachable grandeur, was a worthy object of ambition to an English, a Protestant architect. St Peter's had been built from the religious tribute of the whole Christian world; it might be said, at the cost of a revolution which severed half the world from the dominion of Rome.... St Peter's had been the work of about twenty Popes.... It was its misfortune rather than its boast. That it had commanded the creative powers of many men of the most transcendent genius, who had each his conception and his plan ... St Paul's is the creation of one mind; it is one great harmonious conception.

The long-drawn-out construction of St Peter's was, therefore, marked both by the division of Christendom and by a series of individual architects and differing architectural styles. St Paul's, by contrast, proclaimed a unity both of faith and design. As the Church

Wenceslas Hollar's engraving of old Saint Paul's, from William Dugdale's *The History of Saint Paul's Cathedral* (1658), shows the ancient cathedral without its spire but with the portico added by Inigo Jones c.1634. The statues of James I and Charles I decorating this noble portico were removed during the Commonwealth.

of England had retained its bishops, unlike most other Protestant confessions, the reconstructed cathedral was a declaration of the eminence of the see of London and of a bishop whose jurisdiction covered not only the capital city, but also stretched as far as the new American colonies. St Paul's was, therefore, emphatically a bishop's church rather than, as was to be the case of the great Baroque Frauenkirche in Protestant Dresden, a church built primarily to serve a civic congregation.

London's first St Paul's was constructed in 604 by its first bishop, Mellitus, one of St Augustine's faithful Benedictine companions. It may well have stood on the site of an even earlier Christian building dating from Roman times. Mellitus's church was replaced first by a Saxon minster and then, from 1087, by a huge Norman cathedral.

After a serious fire in the late twelfth century, the Norman cathedral was again enlarged. A new twelve-bay choir, again of gigantic proportions, extended the cathedral further eastwards in the years 1250–1314. So substantial were the piers that once supported the great central tower that when Sir Christopher Wren attempted to clear the ruins of the burnt-out medieval minster in the 1670s he had to resort to gunpowder to bring them down.

Old St Paul's was by far the largest cathedral church in England. It was greater in area than York and Durham, and longer than Winchester. Its extraordinarily handsome lead-covered spire was some thirty feet higher than that of Salisbury. The massive presence of the old cathedral and the wondrous height of its spire sufficiently impressed one anonymous fourteenth-century observer that he or she accurately sketched them on the wall of the tower of Ashwell Church in Hertfordshire. This medieval graffito is not our only visual record of the lost building. Fortunately, shortly before its destruction in the Great Fire of London, Sir William Dugdale published in 1658 a careful account of the history of the cathedral illustrated by a series of excellent and highly informative engravings by the great Czech etcher, Wenceslas Hollar. These plates show the now spire-less cathedral in Cromwellian times. Despite the fact that it has been denuded of many of its most significant medieval fittings, Hollar's plates suggest both its brooding grandeur and the residual magnificence of its proportions.

Hollar's engravings of Old St Paul's also carefully delineate the timely 'restoration' of the cathedral in the 1630s at the capable hands of Inigo Jones. Jones was no 'Gothicist' and the changes he wrought in the character of St Paul's would certainly have been deemed deeply unsympathetic by later generations. But in many ways he preserved the integrity of the great church. He even managed to enhance it. The famous 520-foot high spire had been struck by lightning and destroyed in 1561 (for many Catholics it was a sign of Divine displeasure at Elizabeth I's determined Protestantism). Funds were collected from the City of London and from the Crown to restore the spire, but nothing was achieved beyond repairs to the church's roof. The London historian, John Stow, wryly commented: 'Divers models were devised and made, but little else was done, through whose default, God knoweth; it was said that the money appointed for the new building of the steeple was collected and brought to the hands of Edmond Grendall, then Bishop of London.' This innuendo may well have been Stow's response to the fact that the puritanical Grendall had sent his chaplain to report on the historian's supposedly suspicious collection of 'old fantastical popish books'. Whatever the truth about the failure to reconstruct the cathedral's spire in the 1560s the innuendo was dropped in later editions of Stow's history of London.

In the opening years of the reign of James I, however, the condition of the church as a whole had begun to give cause for grave concern. In March 1620 the King appointed a Royal Commission, on which Inigo Jones served, to report on what could be done to restore the cathedral, but it was not until the reign of Charles I that any firm action was taken. This newly positive response was largely due to the reforming energy of William Laud who served as Bishop of London from 1628–33 (he maintained his support for the campaign of restoration during his troubled time as Archbishop of Canterbury). Charles I himself proved particularly generous, defraying the cost of the superb Classical portico added to the west end of the cathedral. The construction of this portico and the general tidying up of what was probably an unfinished Gothic façade entailed both the demolition of shops and houses that had encroached upon the church and the disappearance of the parish church of St Gregory. The ruthlessness of these demolitions returned to haunt Laud at the time of his trial. Arrogant and tactless Laud might have been, but Jones's portico became for some thirty years one of the new wonders of England, vastly admired even by its ultimate destroyer, Christopher Wren. Puritan anti-Royalists may have toppled the statues of James I and Charles I, which had stood on the portico in the ancient Roman manner, but its noble fluted Corinthian columns withstood the furious heat of the Great Fire in 1666 and remained standing until work began on clearing the site of the old cathedral in preparation for the construction of its successor. Jones's re-ordering of Old St Paul's was perhaps intended to form a monumental climax to a processional route from the Palace of Whitehall to the City. It was thus probably integral to Charles

I's and Laud's vision of the union of the Church of England with the divinely appointed Stuart monarchy. Even for those opposed to Laud's vision of the Church of England the alterations to St Paul's had a deep relevance. In an England where the role of bishops was being rigorously disputed, the restored and semi-Classicized St Paul's may well have been seen as advancing the prestige of a great metropolitan church that might, were episcopacy to be abolished, take precedence over Canterbury.

DISASTER DURING THE GREAT FIRE

Any speculation concerning the future fortunes of the Gothic St Paul's became irrelevant in September 1666 when the cathedral was burnt out during the Great Fire of London. Some eighty-five parish churches suffered the same fate. Samuel Pepys, the most celebrated eyewitness to have recorded his emotions at the time, describes the stones of the cathedral flying 'like grenades' and the molten lead from its roofs 'running down the streets in a stream, and the very pavements glowing with fiery redness, so as no horse or man was able to tread on them'. 'A miserable sight of Paul's Church,' Pepys noted in his diary on Friday 7 September, 'all the roofs fallen in and the body of the quire fallen into St Fayths.' Despite all the efforts expended by those who had attempted to save the building it was evident that the cathedral and the adjoining parish church of St Faith were irreparably wrecked. Curious visitors came to bemoan the loss of a building which had once appeared to have been built to withstand any disaster. The impact of the gigantic ruins must have been akin to that of the melancholy remains of bombed cities after the Second World War. Pepys marvelled at aspects of the terrible wreck of St Paul's, noting in the November of 1666 that the skeletal body of Robert Braybrooke, the Bishop of London who died in 1404, had been toppled out of his broken tomb with remnants of flesh on it 'all tough and dry like a spongy dry leather or touchwood'. The shrivelled corpse 'now exposed to be handled and derided by some, though admired for its duration by others'.

RISING LIKE A PHOENIX

When it came to selecting an architect for the new cathedral Sir Christopher Wren seems to have been the obvious choice. There also seems to have been no doubt that the style of the building should be Classical rather than Gothic. Once in a while the rare parish churches constructed or reconstructed in the Restoration period were built in a style that harked back to the Middle Ages (Charles Church in Plymouth is an example). This choice was probably determined by a desire to suggest the historic roots of the Church of England after the disruptions of the Commonwealth (this late seventeenth-century Gothicism can still be seen in secular buildings such as the Great Hall of Lambeth Palace). No such nostalgia seems to have informed Wren's clear desire to construct a cathedral in the latest Classical (or 'Italian') style with a dome rather than a spire. Shortly before its destruction, Wren had proposed a thorough Classicizing of the Gothic church, crowning its crossing with a spectacular dome topped with an elongated pine-cone. Following the Great Fire all of Wren's designs for the new cathedral show the emergence of increasingly elegant cupolas to crown the new church. In December 1672 Wren's 'Great Model' ('soe large that a Man might stand within it') was shown to Charles II for his approval. This superb oak and pear-wood model is for a centrally planned church with four roughly equal arms stretching out from a circular choir space. There was to be a central dome and a lower, subsidiary dome to the west standing behind a noble portico of eight 50-ft high Corinthian columns. This supremely beautiful 'Great Model' survives to testify to one of the unbuilt masterpieces of English architecture. It can still be admired, for it is displayed in another great masterpiece – the present cathedral.

Although the first, centrally planned design seems to have been approved by Charles II, it fell foul of the cathedral's clergy. It was sometimes claimed in the eighteenth century that Wren's ambitious proposal was blighted by the interference of the Roman Catholic Duke of York (the future James II). James, it was said, believed it unsuited to the kind of Catholic worship he hoped to introduce once he inherited the throne. Nothing could be further from the

The West Front of St Paul's Cathedral, as completed by Sir Christopher Wren in 1708.

truth. It was in fact a group of traditional Anglicans who protested against the shape of a building that they considered 'not enough of a Cathedral-fashion'. By this they meant that a circular choir was not a convenient space for the required daily *Anglican* choral services of Matins and Evensong. They wanted both a dedicated east end of the kind they had been used to in medieval churches and a larger space appropriate for the preaching of public sermons and for state ceremonial (it was only at these ceremonies that congregations of more than five hundred persons were anticipated). The ill-informed modern critics who like to claim that architectural conservatism dictated that the principles exhibited in the 'Great Model' should be rejected also miss the point. The clergy argued for a return to a tradition that had been broken during Cromwell's time and they also wanted an east end cut off by a screen from the more public space of the nave. It should also be remembered that the nave of Old St Paul's (sometimes called 'Paul's Walk') had been a notoriously raucous semi-secular place where civil business was conducted and Londoners strolled and chatted. Wren, the nephew of an Anglican bishop, knew exactly the nature and substance of the dean and chapter's complaints.

The plan that was finally approved in May 1675 is known as the 'Warrant Design'. It may look ungainly to modern observers familiar with the masterpiece that Wren ultimately developed from it, but what should truly strike us is the evidence it offers of the architect's innate sense of practicality and pragmatism. Essentially, the 'Warrant Design' was one that could evolve. The site having been cleared in the interim, and funds raised from a tax on household coals coming into London, a foundation stone was laid in June 1675. Even as work began on the foundations it emerged that Wren had already departed from the proportions and dimensions of the 'Warrant Design'. He continued to alter it even more radically, adding new western towers and gradually perfecting the shape of the dome that would crown the completed cathedral. It is that great dome which continues to distinguish the exterior of the new St Paul's from all other English cathedrals. Nevertheless, like the spire of Salisbury or the Perpendicular central towers of Gloucester and Canterbury, the dome of St Paul's is serene. Unlike the soaring towers of those medieval cathedrals which so characterize distant views of those much smaller cathedral cities, the dome of St Paul's no longer dominates London's skyline. Indeed, it often seems possible to forget that London actually *is* an ancient cathedral city. Nevertheless, Wren's dome has, over the centuries, become the most enduring symbol of London whether it soars over Canaletto's wonderful eighteenth-century cityscapes, or looms through a Dickensian fog, or stands proudly amidst the smouldering ruins left by the Luftwaffe in the 1940s.

The last stone of the new St Paul's was laid by Wren's two sons in October 1708. What is extraordinary is that the 76-year-old Sir Christopher Wren was in attendance at the ceremony. Given the long time-span, and the changes of design that marked the construction of most medieval cathedrals, it is unlikely (though we cannot be certain) that any medieval architect ever saw the fulfilment of the bold designs that they had initiated. St Paul's may have been constructed by a vast teams of surveyors, draughtsmen, engineers, stone-cutters, metal-workers, craftsmen and labourers, but it ultimately stands as the supreme achievement of one man's imaginative genius. Wren's tomb in the cathedral's crypt bears the famous Latin inscription *sic monumentum requiris circumspice* ('if you require a monument, look around you'). There could be no more succinct tribute.

LATER ST PAUL'S

The first worshippers in the newly completed St Paul's Cathedral would still readily recognize its elegant exterior (particularly now that it has been cleaned), but they would be amazed by the transformation of its interior. How precisely Wren might have decorated and fitted its east end we cannot be sure, but he left the rest of the church pristinely bare. Many observant critics found it coldly chaste. Throughout the eighteenth century a great oak choir screen, on which the organ stood, blocked the choir off from the nave and provided the dedicated space the chapter had required for worship. This screen, superbly carved by Grinling Gibbons, was taken down

The choir of St Paul's Cathedral in December 1706, showing the original layout of the choir screen and stalls. This engraving, published in 1710, shows Queen Anne and members of both Houses of Parliament attending a service of thanksgiving. This area of the cathedral was reordered in the mid-nineteenth century and again after the Second World War.

in 1859 when the organ was rebuilt and enlarged. The new vistas temporarily opened up so appealed to the cathedral authorities that they resolved to dismantle the screen, or rather to slice it in half and to re-site it, with one half facing another, in the first bays of the opened-up choir. This radical change in Wren's internal arrangements suggested to the mid-Victorian Dean, Henry Hart Milman, that his cathedral lacked a colourful decorative scheme worthy of its eminent place in national life. When, a hundred years earlier, the founder members of the Royal Academy had proposed to offer their services in providing murals for the cathedral, the then bishop, Richard Terrick (1764–77), dismissed the scheme as savouring of 'Popery' and 'likely to produce clamours' (this was shortly before the anti-Catholic Gordon Riots). No such qualms troubled Dean Milman and his successors. Between 1872 and 1875 the by now dingy surviving colour scheme left by Wren was stripped away and the spandrels of the dome were filled with mosaics of the four Evangelists and four Old Testament prophets. In the 1890s the choir was transformed by a series of glowingly bright mosaics designed by Sir William Blake Richmond. The half dome of the apse contains a particularly striking image of Christ in Glory flanked by recording angels. In 1891 a towering new marble reredos was installed behind a new high altar. The mosaics remain but the reredos, designed by George Frederick Bodley, was removed after sustaining slight damage in the Second World War. It was replaced in the 1950s by a baldacchino carried on four barley-sugar Corinthian columns. This baldacchino, designed by Stephen Dykes-Bower, is derived from a drawing that may well represent Wren's original intention. Unlike the towering Bodley reredos, it allows light to flood into the choir from the eastern windows and responds both to the circumambient architecture and, distantly, to Bernini's vast bronze baldacchino in St Peter's in Rome.

During the last years of the eighteenth and the first half of the nineteenth century, St Paul's was gradually filled with a particularly fine set of sculptured monuments which render it a kind of national pantheon. The cathedral authorities were always acutely aware of a rivalry with Westminster Abbey, both in terms of the national ceremonies it hosted and in terms of the dignitaries who were buried within its walls. This had been as true of the medieval cathedral, but virtually all of the old tombs and monuments were lost irretrievably during the Great Fire of 1666. One particularly celebrated carved monument did somehow survive from the old cathedral; that of its most famous dean, John Donne. Donne's effigy, carved at its subject's request to show the dying dean in his shroud anticipating his resurrection, now stands in the south choir aisle. It was finally placed there in 1873 having formerly been relegated to the crypt (Donne's actual resting place having perished during the Great Fire). Most of the other noble tombs and monuments that so enhance the building were placed there during the nineteenth century. The actual burial places of Nelson and Wellington lie in the crypt, but the elaborate monuments erected to their memory are sited respectively in the South Transept and the North Choir Aisle. The Duke of Wellington's complex Renaissance-style shrine, designed by Alfred Stevens, was only finally completed in 1894. The crowning equestrian statue of the Duke was added very belatedly in 1912.

CATHEDRAL LIFE IN THE EIGHTEENTH CENTURY

It might be argued that the vast cost of rebuilding St Paul's somehow exhausted the possibility of any other great structural initiative being undertaken by the Church of England. There is some truth in this. As no new dioceses were created during the eighteenth century there was no need for a new cathedral church. As no major disaster, akin to the Great Fire of London, befell the existing English cathedrals, no major rebuilding was required. Nevertheless, as we have already seen, a good deal of misguided 'restoration' and reordering took place, mainly thanks to the initiatives of certain wealthy prelates with pretensions to taste. In the last decade of the eighteenth century James Wyatt was employed to work on the cathedrals at Lichfield, Salisbury, Hereford, Durham and Ely. His work might have been considered an act of 'improvement' by his rich employers but it was vigorously condemned by antiquarians and utterly disparaged by later generations. In 1795 Wyatt's candidacy for the Society of Antiquaries was blackballed – it being argued by one member that 'he has destroyed … the ancient sepulchres and monuments which we are associated … to protect [and] by admitting him into our number, we shall appear in the face of our contemporaries and of all posterity to sanction a system which tends to deprive us of the very subjects of our study, and the sources of our information.' Although Wyatt *was* eventually elected to the Society of Antiquaries his detractors succeeded in their long campaign to destroy his reputation as a church restorer. For the Victorian architect, A.W.N. Pugin, Wyatt was quite simply and irredeemably 'the Destroyer'. In the great churches untouched by Wyatt's interventions a Protestant sobriety ruled. Late-seventeenth-century fittings, such as box-pews and three-decker pulpits, were retained because they were regarded as appropriate to the somewhat exclusive celebrations of the Prayer Book services practised by deans and chapters. The only new fittings of any artistic quality were marble sepulchral monuments (the imagery of which tended to be of a decidedly secular nature).

In no sense did eighteenth-century cathedral authorities consider that they were obliged to serve the wider Anglican community of the diocese. Cathedrals were not especially welcoming institutions, particularly if a sacristan or pew-opener found it inconvenient to open a locked building to the interested visitor if that visitor had arrived out of service time. If entry were granted, a tip to the sacristan was always expected. As late as 1856 the novelist George Eliot declined to be 'shown' the inside of Exeter Cathedral by a 'hard, dry-looking woman' and therefore confined her sightseeing to the city streets. Even daily worship in cathedrals tended to be an exclusive business. In the opening chapter of *The Mystery of Edwin Drood* Dickens describes the choir of the fictional Cloisterham Cathedral filing into Evensong and the 'iron-barred gates that divide the sanctuary from the chancel' being firmly locked behind them. St Paul's in London, then as now, was used for state ceremonials, funerals and thanksgivings, but the provincial quiet of most other English cathedrals was rarely disturbed. Notable exceptions were when they were required by the local diocesan to host mass confirmation services or when they provided a religious focus for the annual Assizes (that was, if the cathedral city also served as an assize town).

THE THREAT OF REFORM

By the opening decades of the nineteenth century there was a common public suspicion that cathedral closes were nests of privilege and spiritual laziness rather than enclaves of sober living and active scholarship. Anthony Trollope's *Barchester Towers* (1852) describes the enforced return of Dr Vesey Stanhope, a canon of Barchester Cathedral and the incumbent of three Barsetshire parishes, who has for many years resided on the agreeable shores of Lake Como rather than in his house in the close. As Trollope knew, the duties attached to a well-endowed canonry were rarely onerous but, until his new bishop has insisted on his resumption of them, Dr Stanhope has declined to acknowledge any sense of pastoral responsibility. Where a cathedral chapter's income was very considerable, as was a notorious case at Durham, it was not uncommon for at least one of the twelve non-resident prebends to be bishop of a see that commanded a less impressive income. One of the last so to do was the contentious prelate, Henry Phillpotts. Phillpotts, a prebend of Durham since 1808, retained his lucrative canonry in the North despite being appointed to the distant see of Exeter in 1831. Trollope wryly notes that the High Church archdeacon Grantley of Barchester Cathedral has a bust of Phillpotts in his library!

Disturbed by the national debate on Reform in the late-1820s and early 1830s, the Bishop of Durham resolved to avert further criticism of his cathedral by diverting some of its income to the foundation of a new university in the city and giving his castle over as a college (education being regarded as far more worthy of national respect than quirky ecclesiastical sinecures). That a wider, and possibly yet more radical reform of cathedral establishments was being widely discussed troubled those wedded to the old order of things. In the 1820s the great landscape painter, John Constable, who as friend of Archdeacon Fisher of Salisbury stayed regularly at Fisher's large house in the close, dramatically portrayed what some saw as the threats to cathedral establishments by painting Salisbury Cathedral beset by darks clouds and flashes of lightning. Supposed cathedral 'abuses' were to be investigated by a commission established by the reforming Sir Robert Peel. This commission resulted in a series of Acts of Parliament between 1836 and 1852 which reduced the number of canons in each of the cathedrals to four and insisted that they should be resident for at least three months a year.

Despite the fact that one especially notable cathedral organist, Samuel Sebastian Wesley, cynically told the Cathedral Commissioners in 1854 that 'at least half the number' of the adult male choirmen with whom he had worked were local tradesmen 'who had once or oftener been bankrupt or compounded with their creditors', the tradition of Anglican choral music saw a revival in its fortunes. Following the reports of the Commissioners, cathedral choir schools were re-established on an ordered basis, moulding many of the traditions that continue to flourish into the twenty-first century. There were exceptions to the general impression of decadence. In the western cathedrals of Gloucester, Worcester and Hereford, the great triennial Three Choirs Festival, first established in the early eighteenth century, garnered both a new prestige and a series of highly significant new commissions. The festival, which properly claims to be the oldest non-competitive music festival in the world, offers impressive testimony both to continuity in the life and work of English cathedrals and to a new, and possibly long overdue spirit of renewal

NEW RESPONSES TO CATHEDRAL ARCHITECTURE

What unequivocally altered public responses to English cathedrals in the hundred years between 1720 and 1820 was the quality and diversity of printed accounts of their architecture and history. Some of these texts were of a pioneer archaeological nature. Others contained engraved illustrations of an extraordinary beauty. What is certain is that they steadily rendered the English cathedrals central to perceptions of the historical and aesthetic achievements of the nation. They also signalled a determined shift in taste. By the end of the eighteenth century the various Gothic styles were no longer considered barbaric. By the same token it gradually became more acceptable to view the great cathedrals as the proper inheritance of the Church of England rather than as unfortunate and unwieldy relics of Catholic superstition. Even when stripped of much of their imagery and symbolism the great cathedral churches came to be seen as supreme examples of sublimity in architecture. They were also pronounced to be monuments that suggested the radiant glory of medieval England rather than its superstitious darkness and its architectural ignorance. From the mid-eighteenth century a fascination with the Gothic styles came to complement the widely held scholarly adherence to the Classical architecture of Greece and Rome. By the second decade of the nineteenth century the Gothic style had again become virtually synonymous with the very concept of an English cathedral, whether that church looked to Rome or Canterbury for its allegiance. Only the decidedly Classical St Paul's seems to have remained serenely immune from the assumption.

A full roll-call of key texts in the renewed appreciation of cathedral buildings would be a long one. It is nonetheless proper to single out Browne Willis's truly pioneering *A Survey of the Cathedrals of York, Durham, Carlisle, Manchester, Lichfield, Hereford, Worcester, Gloucester and Bristol* which was published in two volumes in 1727. It was followed three years later by Browne Willis's continuation of his historical analyses: *A Survey of ... Lincoln, Ely, Oxford and Peterborough*. In 1771 James Bentham, a prebendary of Ely, issued his much admired *The History and Antiquities of the Conventual and Cathedral Church of Ely* (a second edition of which appeared in 1812 with sixteen fine engravings). The Catholic antiquarian Bishop John Milner issued his eloquent and influential *Dissertation on the Modern Style of Altering Ancient Cathedrals* in 1798 (it was a strident attack on the work of James Wyatt at Salisbury) before publishing his *History and Survey of the Antiquities of Winchester* in 1798–1801. Notable too are Charles Wild's *Architectural Illustrations* of the cathedrals of Canterbury, York, Lichfield, Chester, Lincoln and Worcester, which was issued between 1807 and 1823, with each volume containing superb aquatints. A further volume of 1830 had no text but contained plates of even finer quality. Perhaps the most accessible of all the illustrated surveys of the great cathedrals is the series of volumes produced by the singularly energetic amateur antiquarian, John Britton, between 1813 and 1835. His fourteen volumes describe Salisbury (1814), Norwich (1816), Winchester (1817), York (1819), Lichfield (1820), Canterbury (1821), Oxford (1821), Wells (1824), Exeter (1826), Peterborough (1828), Gloucester (1829), Bristol (1830), Hereford (1831), and Worcester (1835). Britton's texts may now seem musty and lacking in due analysis but his detailed plans and wonderfully evocative engraved illustrations remain unequalled. The many gifted artists employed by Britton were lucky to have their work exquisitely engraved by equally talented etchers. Britton's task was not an easy one. He complained in the preface to his volume on York Minster that he was 'an humble individual, without fortune, and without any other patronage' who had boldly undertaken a task which was 'arduous, expensive and delicate'. It was this lack of patronage, as well as the cost of his fine illustrations, which seems to have galled him from first to last. In his preface to the Norwich volume he wrote of 'sanguine expectations' being 'very frequently terminated by mortifying disappointment' and that it was only 'some degree of enthusiasm' that had stirred him into action. Before beginning work on Exeter Cathedral, Britton claimed that he wrote to the dean and chapter asking for assistance and co-operation. He received no reply. It was small wonder therefore to find him complaining of being treated with 'pride, superciliousness, and chilling neglect'. When he did finally get permission to do both research and a thorough architectural survey of the cathedral, the process required two long and arduous journeys to a then remote city as well as the cost of employing some eight artists. This, Britton noted, 'occasioned an expense which can hardly ever be returned by a fair sale of the present volume.'

With hindsight it is the work of the artists that Britton employed so effectively that now best conjures up the atmosphere of the great cathedrals in the era immediately before Victorian restorers set to work on yet another series of 'improvements'. This was the era that preceded the advent of popular photographic surveys. Were a modern visitor offered the opportunity of entering one of the great cathedrals of England in the 1830s, he or she might well experience a sense of shock at their starkness and a profound disappointment at their lack of colour and imagery. Britton's etchings are untinted, but even as predominantly grey representations of cathedral interiors they convey the extent to which the ancient architecture is often intruded upon by gratuitously plain modern woodwork. These interiors are not as cluttered as those of contemporary parish churches (there are, for instance, few galleries or three-decker pulpits) but convenient box-pews block medieval stall-work and broken stone altar-pieces are obscured by Classical reredoses. The grey stonework and the subdued browns of the pews is relieved here and there by the velvet curtains that helped protect the members of the choir from draughts. There is no lack of dignity, and little sign of neglect, but a pre-Victorian cathedral contained little in terms of fittings that could be said to delight the eye. For the most part, English cathedrals had been transformed into serviceable settings for an unadorned variety of Anglican worship. Having been built for sacrament and ceremony in the Middle Ages they had been somewhat awkwardly reduced to spaces that were required to proclaim the primacy of the spoken, preached and sung word.

THE CATHEDRAL CITY IN NINETEENTH-CENTURY LITERATURE

TROLLOPE AND THE CATHEDRAL CITY

In an important way the outward appearance of the English cathedrals between the late seventeenth and the early nineteenth centuries reflected the largely genteel, complacent and un-earnest nature of the Church of England. Richard William Church, the High Church dean of St Paul's in the 1870s and 1880s, succinctly criticized the state of Anglican affairs in the pre-Victorian age in his observant study *The Oxford Movement* (1891). By the 1830s, Dean Church argues, Anglicans were 'scarcely adapted to the needs of more stirring times'. Moreover, the disproportion between 'the purposes for which the Church with its ministry was founded and the actual tone of feeling among those responsible for its service had become too great.' Essentially, Church suggests, in the politically and intellectually charged years that followed the French Revolution and the Napoleonic Wars churchmen were afraid of principles and 'the one thing they most shrank from was the suspicion of enthusiasm.' The validity of Dean Church's analysis of the wider Ecclesiastical Establishment is even more true of the narrow world of the cathedral close. Bishops, senior clerics and most members of cathedral chapters were drawn exclusively from the ranks of the aristocracy and the upper gentry. Some owed their promotion to family connections, others to political convenience. It was not just that the younger sons of noblemen found promotion in the Church an easy affair, so too the paths of the sons and grandsons of the upper clergy led to comfortable livings and snug sinecures in cathedral closes. Diocesan bishops, who were appointed by the Crown, were often little more than useful tools of successive governments, and they knew it. As senior members of the House of Lords it was they who were to take much of the blame for the failure of movements to reform the British constitution (as we have seen, the Bishop of Bristol's palace was burnt out during riots in 1830). The upper echelons of the Church all too often looked to antagonistic observers like members of a closed and exclusive club

– a club that had set its face against all aspects of Reform.

The complacent, easy-going, but often politically charged character of an unreformed cathedral close in the first half of the nineteenth century is vividly and wittily evoked in the so-called 'Barchester' novels of Anthony Trollope (1815–82). Trollope was not an insider. He was an official of the General Post Office who emerged as a successful novelist only with *The Warden* (1853) and with its even more popular sequel, *Barchester Towers* (1855). In *An Autobiography* (1883) Trollope claimed that he had conceived of the story of *The Warden* in Salisbury when his official duties had taken him to the city. On one midsummer evening in 1852, he tells us, he spent an hour wandering around 'the purlieus of the cathedral' before pausing to meditate on a little bridge over a branch of the River Avon. He was evidently meditating on the potential of a story about the petty politicking of 'bishops, deans and archdeacon'. By his own admission Trollope 'lived' with his characters for a year before beginning work on the new short novel when he was actually in rural Herefordshire, far away from Salisbury. He later disarmingly claimed that he knew little about the day to day lives of the clergy:

> I may as well declare at once that no one at their [the Barchester novels] commencement could have less reason than myself to presume himself to be able to write about clergymen. I have been often asked in what period of my early life I had lived so long in a cathedral city as to have become intimate with the ways of a Close. I never lived in any cathedral city, except London, never knew anything of any Close, and at that time had enjoyed no peculiar intimacy with any clergyman.

Anthony Trollope may not have actually been on intimate terms with any single clergyman but he is not quite telling the truth about his acquaintance with cathedral cities. As a boy he had spent two and a half unhappy years at Winchester College (which is a short distance from the cathedral). He had also lived in Exeter for a brief period and his Post Office duties had taken him regularly to Bristol, Gloucester, Worcester and Hereford. Barchester, and its surrounding county of Barsetshire, may be figments of Trollope's imagination but it has many of the characteristics of the real counties of Devon, Somerset, Wiltshire, and Hampshire. If the close at Barchester with which Trollope's readers become very familiar is equally an invention it seems to intermix elements of that at Salisbury where the novelist himself confessed to having made out to his own satisfaction 'the spot where Hiram's Hospital should stand'. Despite Trollope's architectural vagueness about the nature of Barchester Cathedral and its close, most readers of the Barchester novels seem to rejoice in identifying elements of an Exeter here and a Winchester there, and a good deal of Salisbury everywhere.

The adjective 'Trollopian' is commonly used to describe the mind-set of the early nineteenth-century Church of England with good reason. As Trollope well knew, the English cathedral city of the nineteenth century was a uniquely English phenomenon. It may have had pale and self-conscious imitations in small Anglican cities in New Zealand and the United States, but these cities were (and are) largely the product of a nostalgia for the 'Old Country' and for an Anglican order which was marginal to predominantly secular colonial constitutions. The English cathedral city was unique because though France, Germany, Spain and Italy possess great medieval cathedrals, no other European country has had a parallel religious and constitutional history. France, Spain and Italy retained their ancient Catholic loyalties during and after the Reformation period and where there were great cathedral establishments these remained under the control of a celibate, secular clergy. They were, of course, exclusively male preserves. In France and the Low Countries the cathedrals and their ancillary buildings were ravaged at the time of the French Revolution. The canons attached to these churches were displaced and very few cathedrals proved able, or willing, to restore the old order of things once the Church re-established its sway. Since Napoleonic times church buildings have been owned and financed by the French State. Given the growth and rabidity of post-Revolutionary anti-clericalism the very idea of a bishop or an archbishop wielding political power would have seemed either preposterous or constitutionally impossible. In Protestant areas of Germany the Lutheran Reformation gradually abolished many historical episcopal sees and the chapters attached to their medieval cathedrals. In some cases the quirky transformation of these chapters took place over a long time span. Those bishops who declared themselves Protestants effectively abolished themselves. In some cathedrals – Halberstadt, for example – Catholic canons continued to live cheek-by-jowl with Protestant ones until well into the seventeenth century, though a predominantly Lutheran culture in northern Germany after the Thirty Years' War saw the gradual elimination of Catholic influence. The fact that eighteenth- and early nineteenth-century Germany consisted of a myriad of small states equally meant that no single Church and its establishment dominated national life. Independent prince-bishoprics survived throughout Germany until Napoleonic times and those still in communion with Rome experienced a cultural reflorescence (at least in terms of their architecture). Nevertheless, with bishop-less Protestant former cathedrals run as parish churches by a married secular clergy, and the surviving Catholic cathedrals generally under the sway of powerful independent prelates, no valid parallel with England can be drawn. Indeed, in Trollope's day the German churches and surviving German cathedral establishments were undergoing yet more radical political and constitutional change.

What drew Trollope to secluded English cathedral closes as the subject of a novel was the fact that they were gossipy, conservative, privileged nests of well-off married clergy. It is virtually impossible to conceive of one of his French or Russian contemporaries writing with such comic zest about the religious communities of their own countries. The word 'Trollopian' is therefore applicable only to England and to an England that was confronting change which was at once social and political. Not only did English cathedral clergy have families and family connections, but many well-placed clergymen hoped to be promoted within the hierarchy and even to aspire to a bishop's throne and, with it, a seat in the House of Lords. Trollope delighted in the fact that major church dignitaries were national rather than simply provincial figures. Having been appointed by the Crown, bishops were regarded by successive prime ministers as useful tools of state. Deans too were Crown appointees and, though vote-less in Parliament, were expected to be acquiescent. At the beginning of *Barchester Towers*, for example, the aged Bishop Grantly dies and his son, the worldly Archdeacon vainly aspires to assume his late father's dignity. It is not to be. Archdeacon Grantly's hopes ('were they innocent or sinful') are dashed when the politically amenable Bishop Proudie is appointed to the vacant see. Proudie, Trollope tells his readers, had already become known as 'a useful and rising clergyman', one who had 'adapted himself to the views held by the Whigs on most theological and religious subjects'. Small-town Barchester's set ways and established Tory prejudices are, we guess, to be shaken by larger political forces. Moreover, the Barchester close has to cope not only with the new Whig bishop but also the most weighty article in the bishop's baggage – his formidable wife.

Trollope seems never to have felt the need to provide Mrs Proudie with a Christian name. She never seems to require one. Intimacy, even with her husband, is remote to her nature. She is well off and well connected, being the niece of a Scottish earl. She assumes that she both out-ranks and out-flanks her spouse. As Trollope cruelly notes, she is 'habitually authoritative to all, but to her poor husband ... despotic.' The novelist never admitted to having based Mrs Proudie on any real bishop's wife, nor would most Victorian readers have assumed that she was the norm of what was expected from the wife of a senior clergyman. What seems to fascinate Trollope in the Barchester novels is the power of women working, as it were, behind the scenes and behind the throne. She is much more than an *eminence grise*. No one in the diocese of Barchester would have dared to deny Mrs Proudie her social status both as a woman of rank and as the wife of their diocesan. Proudie himself might have been 'a sufficiently good bishop,' Trollope wryly remarks in *The Last Chronicle of Barset*, 'had it not been that Mrs Proudie was so much more than a sufficiently good bishop's wife.'

As his political novels about the Palliser family also suggest, Trollope was fascinated by the subtle, but significant, influence exercised by Victorian women. Mrs Proudie can scarcely be described as 'subtle' but she is adept at playing the role of a woman of leisure who declines to be leisured. No particular Victorian woman has emerged as a model for Bishop Proudie's wife, but Trollope was probably well aware of the mission of one particularly remarkable clerical wife: the tireless Evangelical Josephine Butler (1828–1906). Mrs Butler's career as a vocal abolitionist, a determined advocate of women's higher education, and a campaigner against the Sexual Diseases Acts was often assumed to have impeded her husband's clerical promotion (though he was belatedly given a canonry at Winchester in 1882). One remark attributed to her ('God and one woman make a majority') suggests that she was rarely lacking either in self-confidence or self-justification. Josephine Butler's obituary in *The Times* spoke warmly of 'an almost ideal woman: a devoted wife, exquisitely human and feminine, with no touch in her of the "woman of the platform", though with the great gift of pleading speech: with a powerful mind, and a soul purged through with fire.' No Mrs Proudie, therefore, but certainly far from the unassumingly modest model of a Victorian canon's wife.

Cloisterham and Melchester: Dead Sees?

Apart from Barchester two other fictionalized English cathedral cities memorably appear in Victorian novels. Neither of them is shown in a particularly flattering light. Dickens's Cloisterham in *The Mystery of Edwin Drood* (1870) is very obviously based on Rochester, yet despite Dickens's personal attraction to the city, its cathedral is generally characterized in the novel as dank, dusty and death-haunted. Only once, towards the end of the unfinished novel, do we glimpse it flushed briefly with a renewed sense of hope. On a fine summer morning balmy air penetrates into the cathedral, subduing 'its earthy odour' and preaching 'the Resurrection and the Life'. There is no such hope evident in Sue Bridehead's dismissal of the atmosphere of the cathedral at Melchester (Salisbury). When Jude Fawley sentimentally suggests that he and she should sit in the cathedral in Thomas Hardy's blisteringly anti-Christian novel *Jude the Obscure* (1895), he finds little responsive sympathy:

Cathedral? Yes. Though I think I'd rather sit in the railway station ... That's the centre of the town life now. The Cathedral has had its day ... The Cathedral was a very good place four or five centuries ago; but it is played out now ...

Trollope's Barchester is never viewed with quite that degree of cynicism. Trollope disarmingly described himself in his *Auto-biography* as 'an advanced conservative Liberal'. Such a definition might usefully be applied to his various accounts of life in the Close at Barchester. The first of the Barchester novels, *The Warden* suggests, however, that readers might warm to benign and well-meaning representatives of the old order. But change was not only in the air, it had become a pressing political demand. Barchester changes as we observe it. In a classically English, even classically *Anglican* way, the cathedral city adjusts to change and adapts to new political, intellectual and spiritual demands. Despite what Hardy's Sue Bridehead proclaims, the English cathedral was not 'played out' by the end of the Victorian Age. On the contrary, with a large number of new cathedrals, many of them *not* Anglican cathedrals, the life of the great churches of the land was witnessing a resurgence which helped to subdue 'the earthy odour' of the old and (to some observers) a redundant, world.

5

THE VICTORIAN CATHEDRALS

WHEN ST AUGUSTINE SOUGHT advice from Pope Gregory at the beginning of his mission to England the Pope advised that he should establish two provinces: one in the south centred in Canterbury, and one in the north centred on York. Each ecclesiastical province would cover ten dioceses. Although the two archbishoprics survive to this day, the equal division of the island into ten northern and ten southern sees was never properly realized. Augustine's mission met with setbacks and political complications. Anglo-Saxon kingdoms vied with one another or, having accepted Christianity, reverted to paganism. Early bishops found themselves at best without sees or at worst in exile. Even so, in the more settled state of late-Saxon England the province of Canterbury embraced far more sees than the northern province. Very little had changed in terms of the number and distribution of dioceses by the start of the Victorian era.

Although some medieval archbishops of York had hoped that their authority stretched into Scotland, their pretensions were finally quashed when, in the late fifteenth century, Rome acknowledged the full independence of the Scottish Church by creating two archbishops at St Andrews and Glasgow. Until the 1830s the Province of York contained within it just four large dioceses (York, Chester, Carlisle and Durham) and the much smaller see known as 'Sodor and Man' (which, having long lost the Scottish islands under its authority, covered only the Isle of Man). The Province of Canterbury, by contrast, contained the long-established sees of Canterbury, Rochester, London, Winchester, Chichester, Salisbury, Exeter, Wells, Bristol, Gloucester, Worcester, Hereford, Lichfield, Oxford, Peterborough, Ely, Norwich, and Lincoln. It also exercised authority over the four Welsh sees (an authority it only lost when the Anglican Church in Wales was disestablished in 1914). Even Henry VIII's creation of new sees in the sixteenth century had done little to correct the imbalance between north and south. Although in terms of wealth and population the south had always predominated, the distribution of population had begun to shift radically thanks to the eighteenth-century Industrial Revolution. In the late Middle Ages Lincoln, Norwich, Winchester, Salisbury, and Exeter were all substantial cities. Money, industry and people remained concentrated in the south until around 1700. Thereafter all three determinants of power either moved north or exploded in already established cities. The population of Salisbury was about 10,000 in 1840 and it had only risen by another 3,000 thirty years later. Winchester had only 14,000 citizens in the 1850s and as late as 1881 had only expanded to 19,500. In the same year, according to the National Census, Chichester boasted a mere 7,842 inhabitants, Ely some 10,000, Exeter 37,000 and Worcester 44,000. By contrast, Manchester's population stood at around 500,00 in 1870 and nearly 570,000 ten years later. The population of Liverpool was some 611,000 in 1881, that of Birmingham 435,000, that of Leeds 309,000 and that of Newcastle 150,000.

It was not just changes in population density that finally forced the hand of the political and ecclesiastical Establishment. In 1828 the last civil disabilities were removed from the now large body of English Nonconformists. In 1829 the Catholic Emancipation Act gave full civil liberties to the much smaller, but historically much more persecuted, community of English Roman Catholics. The 1832 Reform Act had not only extended the franchise but also redistributed parliamentary seats, thus giving representation to the burgeoning cities of the north. Sensing that an extended reformist agenda initiated by the new Whig government might threaten the status quo, many churchmen began to fear the worst. As we have seen in in Chapter 4, in 1830 Bishop Van Mildert of Durham transferred cathedral endowments and his castle to the university he had founded. In 1833 the Whig government suppressed certain sees in the sister Protestant Church of Ireland. Although the historic endowments of these sees were to be reused for social and educational purposes, this action persuaded one prominent cleric, the Reverend John Keble, to preach a sermon at Oxford. This sermon was published with the title 'National Apostasy'. Keble's sermon called the Church to political action and for spiritual renewal and self-assertion. It came to be regarded by many as the trumpet-call for what became known as the 'Oxford Movement'. The Church, Keble argued, had both historic roots and a divinely ordained mission and should be exempt from political tampering, however well-meaning.

THE NEW ANGLICAN SEES IN THE NORTH

RIPON

It is in the light of these changes in the body politic that we can sense the significance of the establishment in 1836 of the first new Anglican see in three centuries. The ancient Minster of Ripon was raised to the rank of a cathedral with its bishop, C.T. Longley, administering a new diocese carved out of the archdiocese of York. The bishopric embraced much of the old North Riding of Yorkshire but included the city of Leeds. Ripon Minster, with its strong links to the mission of St Wilfred in the seventh century, contains a particularly moving crypt which had once formed part of Wilfred's cathedral. This sometime cathedral had been relegated to the status of a collegiate church by the twelfth century and lost even that distinction in the reign of Edward VI (its 'collegiate' status being restored by James I). Thus degraded, the minster entered a period of neglect. Work had ceased on rebuilding the crossing, and the three timber and lead spires that once crowned the towers were destroyed in the seventeenth century. Nevertheless, Bishop Longley's throne was placed in a noble church, anciently rooted in national and local history. The cathedral was, however, situated in a small market town rather than in the nearby industrial Leeds. A suitably grand mansion, in the Tudor style, was

The West Front of Ripon Cathedral.

built to house the bishop in 1841 and the church underwent a thorough restoration at the hands of Sir George Gilbert Scott in the years 1862–70 (it was Scott who removed the cheapskate plaster vault in the nave which had been put up in 1829). Ripon's fortunes as a small and attractive cathedral have see-sawed yet again. At Easter 2014 Ripon lost its distinct episcopal status and its bishops their title. The see, which had already been renamed 'Ripon and Leeds' became part of a new diocese officially, but clumsily, titled 'West Yorkshire and the Dales'. This new diocese also incorporates two other now suppressed sees: Wakefield (founded in 1888) and Bradford (founded in 1919). The Anglican Bishop of Leeds (as he is likely to be known) shares his title with a Roman Catholic diocesan. Unlike his Catholic counterpart, however, he has three cathedrals, for Ripon, Wakefield and Bradford retain their old titles, if not all of their Victorian functions.

MANCHESTER

The fifteenth-century collegiate church of St Mary, St Denys and St George at Manchester was raised to cathedral status in 1847. The church, which stands overlooking what was in 1847 the polluted and murky River Irwell, was in the very centre of the city, but to many Victorian commentators it remained 'a very fine parish church' rather than a building worthy of the name of 'cathedral'. Murray's *Handbook to the Northern Cathedrals* of 1869 carped that 'the church possesses none of the features which ought to mark the cathedral of a great see, and which do mark every English Cathedral of the older foundations.' Even had there been the will and the resources to reconstruct or expand the existing building in a grander manner there was no available open space to its east. Manchester's first bishop, James Prince Lee, had a daunting enough task in administering a diocese which embraced all of industrial Lancashire apart from the city of Liverpool (which remained in the see of Chester).

Before his elevation to the episcopate, Lee's background had been in education. He had been Master at Rugby School and Headmaster of King Edward's School at Birmingham. He proved to be a good bishop, but scarcely a great one (he was dogged with unfounded accusations of drunkenness). The populous city to which he was appointed was approaching the zenith of its wealth, though it was also beset with dire problems of poverty, appalling housing and notoriously bad sanitation. The emphatic Anglican presence represented by the new bishopric was of great symbolic significance, but industrial Manchester had long ceased to be an exclusively Anglican city. The diocese contained a large number of Roman Catholics, Lancashire's residual Catholic population having been swelled by recent Irish immigration. Manchester itself had also long been famous as a centre of Dissent (the city contained four Methodist circuits, four Unitarian, five Baptist and eleven Independent chapels). The Cross Street Unitarian Chapel in the centre of Manchester (where William Gaskell, the husband of the novelist Elizabeth Gaskell, was minister) had several prominent members of the city's corporation as congregants. In 1875 as an act of Nonconformist assertion a statue of Oliver Cromwell (no lover of the Church of England) was erected near the cathedral, supposedly on the spot where the first victim of the English Civil War had been killed.

Nevertheless, Manchester has always been justly proud of its handsome cathedral, representing as it does the most significant architectural element of its pre-industrial heritage. When its elegant western tower was rebuilt on a new scale in 1864 the cathedral was also able to assert its presence amid the mills and warehouses that once hemmed it in. Late in the nineteenth century the south-western portion of the nave was reconstructed and in 1897 a new porch was added to mark Victoria's Diamond Jubilee. Despite bomb damage during the Second World War, subsequent schemes of restoration have rendered the interiors of Manchester Cathedral a commodious, dignified and singularly agreeable space.

A NEW CATHEDRAL AND THE ELEVATION OF TWO PARISH CHURCHES

TRURO

When the new sees of Ripon and Manchester were created there was governmental consternation over the fact that new bishops might unbalance the Constitution by increasing the representation of the Established Church in the House of Lords. The problem was temporarily solved, or fudged, when the diocese of Bristol was united to that of Gloucester and a proposal was considered to merge the Welsh sees of St Asaph and Bangor. Nevertheless, despite the steady increase in the population, it took nearly thirty years before another Anglican bishopric was established. In 1876 a Diocese of Truro was created, detaching the county of Cornwall from the see of Exeter. The new see also restored the ancient dignity of a bishopric lost

Truro Cathedral from the east, showing the surviving sixteenth-century aisle and the central tower designed by J.L. Pearson and built in the closing years of the nineteenth century.

to Cornwall since 1043. Such an innovation had long been seen as desirable given the remoteness of much of the county.

The first Bishop of Truro was the intelligent and highly energetic Edward White Benson (later promoted to the archbishopric of Canterbury). Benson, who possessed both a discriminating taste for Gothic architecture and a determination that he should have a new cathedral worthy of his see, set up a committee in 1877 and invited seven prominent architects to submit designs. Truro was not the first new Anglican cathedral to be built to the designs of an eminent nineteenth-century architect (the wonderful St Fin Barre's in Cork in Ireland, St Mary's in Edinburgh, and several fine colonial buildings preceded it), but its importance for contemporaries lay not only its stately and balanced proportions but in the fact that it fulfilled the Victorian ambition to construct a great church that could properly rival the triumphant medieval minsters. As it grew, Truro Cathedral came to dominate and transform the surrounding city. The winning architect, J.L. Pearson, was both fascinated with the intricate vaulting systems of the early Middle Ages in England and deeply attracted by the soaring thirteenth-century stone spires of the churches he had studied in northern Normandy. As a consequence, the new cathedral, like that at Coutances in Normandy, has three towers each crowned with a singularly elegant stone spire. Despite this emphatically Norman outline, Pearson chose an elegant Early English style for most of the building, but perfected it with a consistent sexpartite vault that shows a debt to French precedent. He also retained the sixteenth-century south aisle of the old parish church of St Mary. The spired western towers were finished only in 1910. Alas, Pearson's proposed cloister and chapter house were never built. Instead, an unpleasantly clumsy concrete Memorial Hall of 1967 intrusively jars against the otherwise cool Gothic harmony of the rest of the cathedral.

Bishop Benson commissioned his new cathedral partly because he considered Truro's existing parish church inadequate and unworthy of the dignity of his Cornish see. His ambition to firmly establish his new see went further than architecture. Even with a half-built church he had also begun to pioneer the proper ceremonial and dignified, innovative, liturgical worship of the kind we now generally associate with cathedrals. In 1880, with its newly established choir, Truro hosted the first Christmastide service of 'Nine Lessons and Carols' some thirty-eight years before King's College at Cambridge adopted a similar celebration.

NEWCASTLE-UPON-TYNE

After the establishment of the Cornish diocese a new and positive energy seems to have inspired the creation of five more sees, all of them in populous areas of England. A bishopric, carved out of the northern part of the diocese of London, was founded at St Albans in 1877. Liverpool followed in 1880, Newcastle-upon-Tyne in 1882, Southwell in 1884, and Wakefield in 1888. The new Bishops of Liverpool, Wakefield and Newcastle placed their episcopal thrones in central and distinctly urban parish churches. In Liverpool the late seventeenth-century St Peter's, a box of a building in Church Street (now demolished), was adopted as a merely 'provisional' cathedral. Liverpool's first bishop, J.C. Ryle, was known to be a man who considered cathedrals and their establishments an historical anomaly and largely irrelevant to the modern world. Nevertheless, by 1884 there were plans to build afresh on the site of St John's Church, adjacent to St George's Hall, but the project fell into abeyance and a new, elevated and truly splendid site was selected in 1901. The magnificent cathedral constructed there over a long period will be discussed in the next chapter.

Newcastle's large parish church of St Nicholas was selected to serve as the cathedral of the northernmost diocese in England and one that separated Northumberland from the extensive see of Durham. Ironically, King Edward VI's Protestant council had resolved to create a new cathedral here in 1553 and Parliament had accordingly passed an act to establish a dean and chapter. One of the prime candidates for the proposed bishop was none other than the Scots reformer, John Knox – not a man known to be friendly to the very idea of bishops. Perhaps fortuitously, the plan to promote Newcastle's ecclesiastical fortunes collapsed with the death of the king. Nor were they revived by his immediate successors. Newcastle's first bishop, Ernest Wilberforce, inherited a prominent church with a conspicuously beautiful crowned steeple at its west end. St Nicholas's Church had been rigorously 'restored' in the late eighteenth century and, apart from a careful rebuilding of the tower by Sir Gilbert Scott, the only changes to the interior since it became a cathedral have been largely cosmetic. These consist of a new high altar and reredos, a stone pulpit, a rood screen and choir stalls – all in a sympathetic late Gothic style worked to designs by the gifted Newcastle architect R.J. Johnson.

WAKEFIELD

Before All Saints Church at Wakefield in West Yorkshire was given cathedral status it had been given a particularly thorough and generally adept restoration by Gilbert Scott between 1858 and 1870. At that time the western tower was re-cased and the spire rebuilt and raised in height. Although Scott had also repaired both the nave and the chancel, removing all of their eighteenth-century fittings, by 1897 the old chancel was deemed to be inadequate and J.L. Pearson was called in to design a much grander, stone-vaulted east end rendered much more spacious by well-lit transepts. As at Truro, this work was completed after the architect's death by Pearson's son, Frank, in the years 1901–5. The new sanctuary, with its elaborate reredos, its delicate rood screen and its rich collection of refined stained glass designed by C.E. Kempe, conformed to the highest principles of late Victorian Anglo-Catholicism. Wakefield, like its sisters at Ripon and Bradford, is now one of the three 'cathedrals' of the new Diocese of Leeds.

Southwell Minster

The new bishops of Southwell and St Albans inherited far grander churches than those of Liverpool, Newcastle and Wakefield. The great church at Southwell was, and is, commonly known as 'Southwell Minster'. It was an archbishop's church, attached to the archbishop of York since the tenth century, and by the twelfth century it had become an independent, and rich, collegiate church endowed with lands that covered about one quarter of Nottinghamshire. The pre-Reformation archbishops of York retained a substantial palace here. Most of the building was destroyed during the Civil War, but its ruinous western half was incorporated into the Arts-and-Crafts palace built for the new bishops by the architect W. D. Caröe in 1907–9.

Externally, Southwell Minster, with its two Romanesque western towers capped with lead pyramid-like roofs, resembles a German cathedral rather than an English one. Although these roofs were reconstructed in 1880, they are said to mark a return to their ancient configuration. The minster has a noble, seven-bay Romanesque nave closed at the crossing by a stone pulpitum, or rood screen, built in the mid-thirteenth century and decorated with exquisite and luxuriant ogee arches and crocketed gables. The same masons

Carved in the late thirteenth century, this foliage capital is from the vestibule to the chapter house at Southwell Minster.

were responsible for the much-restored sedilia in the choir. This vaulted choir, in the purest Early English style, was reconstructed by Archbishop de Gray in the years 1234–41. What most distinguishes Southwell is its chapter house. Built in the late thirteenth century, its proportions are relatively small compared to those at Salisbury or Wells, and it has no central column from which its vaults spring. The chapter house is approached by a vestibule and doorway decorated, as are the capitals in the polygonal space beyond, with exquisitely naturalistic carvings of foliage – maple, oak, hawthorn, ranunculus, vine, ivy, and hop. If you look carefully, here and there small animals peep out. It is sculptural work of a quality that has few rivals in England.

When the diocese of Southwell was established in 1884 there was a debate as to whether the see should have been more properly sited in nearby Nottingham (which had a population of some 230,000). When a vote was taken, tiny Southwell proved to have the edge – perhaps because it had recently been munificently and privately endowed. Nevertheless, the new bishop, George Ridding, somewhat ungenerously

Carving of a Green Man in the chapter house at Southwell Minster.

remarked: 'What is the good of a cathedral in a village?' Bishop Ridding's statement indicates how very far Anglican opinion had changed since the twilight days of Barchester.

ABBEY CHURCH OF ST ALBANS

By the middle years of the nineteenth century the market town of St Albans, well connected to nearby London by three railway lines, was certainly no village. When its abbey was raised to the status of a cathedral in 1877 St Albans automatically became a city. The diocese was carved out of what had once been the northern part of the see of London, though since 1836 the counties of Hertfordshire and Essex had somewhat absurdly been given to Rochester (the north Kentish see on the south side of the Thames). The new cathedral city at the core of the diocese possessed an extraordinarily long Christian history. Some claimed that it was the site of unbroken Christian worship since Roman times. St Albans, which once housed the relics of the proto-martyr of England, a Roman soldier executed for his faith in the third century, was, until the Reformation, the premier abbey of England. It had been allotted that honour in 1154 by Adrian IV, the English Pope, who had spent his early years in the monastery. It is significant, therefore, that the cathedral's official title remains that of 'Cathedral and Abbey Church'. Though many visitors assume that it has always been the seat of a bishop, the abbey church was already eight hundred years old when its first bishop was installed. Thomas Legh Claughton was translated here from the see of Rochester, where he had already served as bishop for ten years; or rather, he continued his service in what had been the northern part of his former diocese.

The great church remains a testimony to the architectural ambitions of its first Norman abbot, Paul of Caen, who rebuilt his church using a great deal of ancient red brick salvaged from the remains of the Roman city of Verulamium. Abbot Paul's church was belatedly consecrated in 1116 in the presence of Henry I and his wife, the Archbishop of Rouen, and the Bishops of London, Durham, Lincoln and Salisbury. The already large church was extended by thirteen

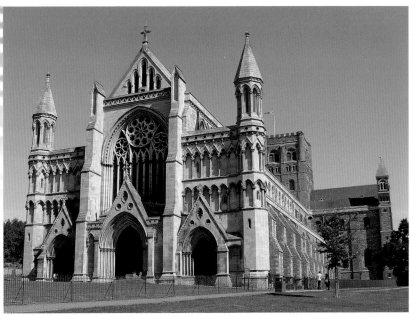

Lord Grimthorpe designed the west front of St Albans Cathedral in 1888.

bays in 1195, but the speed with which work proceeded led to structural weaknesses which became evident by the fourteenth century.
They manifested themselves again in the nineteenth. Nevertheless,
the church as we see it today, with its spacious Norman nave, its
thirteenth-century choir, presbytery and sanctuary, and its singularly beautiful Lady Chapel, is the second longest in England
(only Winchester is longer). From the sixteenth century onwards,
however, it was to suffer grievously. Cardinal Wolsey was elected
abbot in 1526, holding the title with that of the archbishopric of
York. Wolsey benefited handsomely from the income but otherwise did nothing either for or at the abbey. In 1539 the monastery
was surrendered to the Crown and the great church was sold to
the town for £400. It was at this period that the relics of St Alban
were dispersed and the elaborate shrine that contained them was
mutilated and dismantled. Apart from the great gatehouse, the monastery's sprawling buildings were gradually demolished. In 1553,
however, a charter of Edward VI established a grammar school in
the old Lady Chapel. The Lady Chapel was then detached from the

body of the church by a public passageway. The school only moved out in 1869, taking over the gatehouse as its new home, and the chapel was re-incorporated into the body of the great church.

The present cathedral's three centuries as the gargantuan parish church of a small town did little to enhance its state of repair. The brick central tower, which contained a ring of bells and was formerly crowned by a slim spire, was found to be in perilous condition in 1830. The ringing of the bells was prohibited as a precaution against collapse and the spire removed. The tower was shored up, only for its weak foundations to cause serious problems again in 1871. In 1856, however, a 'National Committee' had managed to raise the not inconsiderable sum of £30,000 by subscription and Sir Gilbert Scott was commissioned to undertake a thorough restoration. When Scott died in 1878 the work was incomplete and the funds raised had dried up. It was only thanks to the generosity and private ambition of Sir Edmund Beckett QC that repair work was resumed.

Beckett, who was later created Lord Grimthorpe, had made his fortune by handling the legal affairs of railway companies. He is reputed to have spent some £130,000 of his own money on

The nave of St Albans Cathedral is one of the longest in England.

furthering what he probably considered to be a sympathetically beautiful scheme of 'restoration'. Grimthorpe, who fancied himself as an amateur architect with a particular penchant for 'correct' Gothic, was granted unlimited power 'to restore, repair, and refit the church'. His timely intervention is still a matter of celebration, for he saved the tottering abbey church, but, alas, the heavy-handed mangling of the building has proved to be an aesthetic disaster. It is perhaps the ugliest and most inept restoration of any great medieval building. Like many of his better-informed contemporaries Grimthorpe considered the Early English and Decorated styles the only acceptable ones. He consequently had an unfortunate distaste for any additions to St Albans in what was considered the 'debased' Perpendicular style of the fifteenth and sixteenth centuries. The west front of the old abbey was no model of good architecture, but Grimthorpe's wholesale rebuilding of it is assertively ugly. It is now a dreadful parody of the arcaded façades of Salisbury or Lincoln, with the old nine-light Perpendicular western window replaced by one in a heavy Early English style. Even worse is the treatment of the north and south transepts. To the north, a large fifteenth-century window was replaced by a travesty of a 'rose window' with crude tracery which was often fondly thought to resemble the old polygonal 'threepenny' bits. In 1989 its ugliness was relieved by the insertion of brightly non-representational stained glass. The south transept is rudely punctured by five lancet windows, none of which could originally be appreciated from the inside due to the low pitch of the ceiling (the ceiling has now been raised). One contemporary remarked of this part of the church that 'it would not do credit to a Salvation [Army] barracks'. Grimthorpe seems to have been impervious to such criticism. Given his legal background he was prepared to defend his ground in courts of law. In the late 1890s the fifteenth-century altar screen was repaired at the expense of Lord Aldenham who sought to replace its long-lost statues of saints with new ones. Grimthorpe objected violently to the restoration of the statue of the crucified Christ at its centre and brought a case against Aldenham. Blessedly, Aldenham won on a technicality. An eighteenth-century painted altarpiece of the Last Supper having been removed from above the altar, a commission was given in

1900 to the great late-Victorian sculptor, Alfred Gilbert, to produce a marble image of the Resurrection. Gilbert never completed it (this was not an uncommon aspect of his career). What we have now is extraordinary enough, however: a shrouded Christ, supported by winged angels, rises from the tomb, and two great hands lift the crown of thorns from his head. The angels' wings are covered in iridescent shells which, like the accompanying glass inlay, subtly shimmer in the light.

The history of St Albans Cathedral since Grimthorpe's death in 1905 is far happier. Some fragmentary remains of the Purbeck marble base of Saint Alban's shrine had been discovered when the central arches of the then detached Lady Chapel were opened up. They had been randomly used as in-filling. In 1872 more substantial fragments were found in the south aisle enabling Sir Gilbert Scott to supervise some kind of reconstruction. What resulted was, according to Scott, 'the most marvellous restitution that ever was made.' This, the base of the early fourteenth-century shrine, was placed where it had anciently stood behind the high altar guarded, as it had been in pre-Reformation days, by the wooden watching loft (where monks had supervised the circulation of pilgrim visitors). A careful late-twentieth-century reconfiguration of these carved fragments and a recent substitution of what was once the gold feretory (the actual container of the relics) have restored to this space something of its ancient honour. In 1982 the cathedral opened its new red-brick chapter house to the south of the church, admirably reflecting elements of a Roman basilica. This new building has also given the church the kind of public areas regarded as essential to its modern mission as the host of pilgrims and parishioners alike.

VICTORIAN RESTORATIONS

Lord Grimthorpe's crudely insensitive mauling of the ancient abbey at St Albans blessedly proved to be one of the last examples of Victorian 'over-restoration'. In the 1850s John Ruskin had eloquently expressed his horror at the damage done to historical buildings in Venice by zealous modern architects, and had gone on to remind his fellow-countrymen of the dangerous temptation to opt for 'improvement' over preservation. Ruskin's disciple, William Morris, was moved in 1877 to found the Society for the Preservation of Ancient Buildings, an organization dedicated both to the principles of scrupulous conservation and to active propaganda. Morris's national campaign succinctly summed up its mission as 'anti-scrape' for it was determined to argue that the wholesale replacement of stonework destroyed not only the patina of old buildings but also irreplaceably severed a physical link with the past. Old carved stones bore the marks of the tools of masons and long-dead craftsmen; new stones only spoke of the modern age. Morris, in his forthright way, saw Gilbert Scott as the arch 'scraper', pronouncing after the architect's death that the church at Bradford-on-Avon had been 'scraped to death by G. Scott the (happily) dead dog'. Scott had not in fact been involved in the restoration of Bradford-on-Avon, but he *was* responsible for drastic, and generally timely, architectural interventions at no fewer than twenty English cathedrals (including those at Ely, Chichester, Lichfield, Exeter, and Hereford). Criticized though he was by men of Morris's kidney, most of Scott's work had been exceptionally well received in his lifetime. In 1863, for example, the *Hereford Journal* hailed the 'great work' of restoration at Hereford Cathedral, rejoicing in the fact that 'the building, the mutilating, and repairing eras' were now over. The writer went on:

> The history of the restoration at Hereford Cathedral is, in reality, a history of the revival and progress of ecclesiastical art during the last five-and-twenty years. That is a short period, but it has sufficed for bringing about an entire revolution in the long neglected study of Gothic architecture.

The 'informed' restoration of ancient churches was celebrated because it made manifest the aesthetic achievement of a proud and discriminating modern nation. After two and a half centuries of neglect, and of what was deemed to be an unhappy predisposition to Classical architecture, the middle years of the nineteenth century had witnessed a great revival of the Gothic. Victorian architects were certainly familiar with Italian, French, Spanish and German Gothic

Sir Gilbert Scott's choir screen from Hereford Cathedral *in situ*. The screen was made by F.A. Skidmore and was exhibited in London in 1862. In 1967 it was ejected by the cathedral authorities and can now be seen in the Victoria and Albert Museum.

buildings, but above all else they understood the distinctiveness of the medieval English styles. They not only knew their architectural history, they were determined to show the extent to which they were steeped in the Gothic spirit by reconfiguring churches. At their worst, architects like Grimthorpe ruthlessly stripped away the features they disliked (mostly late medieval tracery) and replaced them with what they considered to more 'correct' details. At their best, the Victorian restorers of cathedrals propped up tottering aisles, secured foundations, and reinforced collapsing towers and spires. They left the structures of the great English cathedrals physically secured for the future. For the most part they left them in the form that we recognize today. Though we may properly regret elements of the process of tampering, altering and scraping, nonetheless we should honour the Victorian enterprise that secured and enhanced a series of irreplaceable architectural masterpieces.

If the act of preservation should be honoured, so too should the transformation of the interiors of the English cathedrals. In the middle years of the twentieth century a huge prejudice against Victorian fittings meant that they were denigrated. At best they were despised and at worst destroyed. We have already noted the removal of Gilbert Scott's reredos at Exeter, the disposal of his screen at Hereford (which is now one of the glories of the Victoria & Albert Museum in London) and the utterly philistine destruction of the reredos and the similar screen at Salisbury. The loss of this last object was an act worthy of the most zealous Puritan iconoclast. From the 1920s to the 1970s Victorian fittings were manifestly not in fashion, but ill-informed deans and chapters seem to have forgotten that the English cathedrals in their charge were spaces on which each century had left a distinct mark. Very few of the great churches were in a consistent architectural style, and even assiduous Victorian restorers had retained 'intrusive' late-medieval chantries and inappropriately elaborate examples of Jacobean or Georgian monumental sculpture. Though Gilbert Scott scrupulously removed seventeenth-century box pews, Classical reredoses and three-decker eighteenth-century pulpits (or at least their sounding boards), he did so because he regarded them as improper in a Gothic building and inconvenient to modern cathedral worship. What he put in their place were often masterly re-inventions of medieval forms which he and his ecclesiastical clients recognized as edifying in themselves and as objects necessary to dignified worship. They were also regarded as a delight to the eye of the modern worshipper.

Many of Scott's finest ensembles of sculpture, metalwork, woodwork, stained glass and encaustic floor tiles have been destroyed or reconfigured. In their own time these fittings exhibited the finest craftsmanship available. As Scott himself remarked of his close associate, the metalworker Francis Skidmore of Coventry, he was 'the only man living ... who was capable of effecting [my designs] and who has worked out every species of ornament in the true spirit of ancient models.' One cathedral, Worcester, has however retained a particularly impressive set of Scott fittings in its choir. The cathedral was in a state of considerable disrepair when a drastic 'restoration' was undertaken by the architect A.E. Perkins in 1857. The exterior detailing of the cathedral as we still see it is very substantially to Perkins's design. Scott was not involved until 1864, by which time

Perkins had replaced the great east window with a double layer of five lancets and taken out the despised Perpendicular tracery in the transept windows. Less intrusively, he had removed layers of whitewash and disposed of the old choir screen, the organ and all of the fittings in the choir. Scott claimed to have regretted many of these changes but he was allowed a free hand in refurnishing the now empty choir and presbytery. The choir vault, which had been laid bare, was re-plastered and decorated by John Hardman under Scott's supervision. Hardman's firm was also responsible for the new stained glass in the windows of the eastern part of the cathedral. Scott provided designs for an opulent stone reredos carved by the firm of Farmer and Brindley at a reputed cost of £1,500. His, too, are the Bishop's Throne, the organ cases and the stalls which incorporate thirty-seven medieval misericords. The floor was re-laid with modern coloured tiles and the magnificent open, oak and metal choir screen was constructed by Skidmore's firm. The choir is thus almost entirely a Victorian creation and it is notable for its subdued and unequalled richness. Now that so much of the prejudice against Victorian architectural innovation has dissipated, the interiors of Worcester Cathedral can be appreciated for the wonder that they are.

CATHOLICISM RESURGENT

Since the middle of the nineteenth century in England the word 'cathedral' could not be applied exclusively or accurately to churches belonging to the Church of England. After some necessary delay, on 29 September 1850, Pope Pius IX published an Apostolic Letter announcing the Restoration of the Roman Catholic Hierarchy in England and Wales. English Catholics had long assumed that the ancient sees of England had been usurped by Protestant state appointees – schismatics who owed no allegiance to Rome. They were therefore neither true bishops nor proper claimants to historic sees established by the universal church. English Catholics had not lacked English bishops, but those superintending bishops having first been obliged to live in exile on the Continent had latterly been known as 'Vicars Apostolic' presiding over districts rather than defined dioceses. In Rome's eyes they were properly consecrated bishops who bore the titles of exotic and long-lost Catholic sees in Asia Minor. The first such, William Bishop was consecrated Bishop of Chalcedon in 1623. Bishop Richard Challoner, the energetic co-adjutor of London in the late eighteenth century was titular Bishop of Debra. The first Archbishop of Westminster, Nicholas Wiseman, had until 1850 been splendidly known as the bishop of Melipotamus. In 1840 the number of Vicars Apostolic had risen to eight but, given the changing circumstances of English Catholics (the Catholic Emancipation Act had allowed the faithful full civil liberties and their numbers had begun to swell, particularly in the North), a more permanent diocesan system was deemed to be an urgent necessity. Unfortunately, that urgency had to be put on hold in 1848 when the Pope was obliged to leave Rome and retreat into a two-year exile. Restored to his dignity, Pius IX again turned his sights to the new province of England and Wales, establishing a metropolitan see at Westminster and twelve further bishoprics: Southwark, Hexham, Beverley, Liverpool, Salford, Clifton, Plymouth, Nottingham, Birmingham, Northampton, Shrewsbury, and Menevia (these last two covering Wales). Some of these sees had historic titles, such as Beverley, Hexham and Menevia (the ancient name for St David's). Others (Birmingham and Liverpool) were named for new cities, yet others for what were effectively subsidiary areas of great cities (Southwark in London, Salford in Manchester). None attempted to echo existing Anglican titles (Liverpool, Birmingham and Southwark were not yet Anglican sees). It was to be Westminster and not London, Salford and not Manchester, Clifton and not Bristol. Significantly, however, though these new bishops had dioceses, only a handful of them had any church in which to place his *cathedra* that was actually worthy of the name of 'cathedral.'

Nicholas Wiseman had been created a cardinal in Rome on 30 September 1850 and a week later published a pastoral letter somewhat pompously entitled 'From out of the Flaminian Gate'. This gate was the main exit to the north from the city of Rome, but Wiseman's letter announcing his departure for England contained what were interpreted as inflammatory, pompous and inappropriate claims. As Archbishop of Westminster, with temporary charge of the Southwark diocese, he would 'govern and shall continue to govern the counties of Middlesex, Hertford and Essex ... and those of Surrey, Sussex, Kent, Berkshire and Hampshire, with the islands annexed, as administrator with ordinary jurisdiction.' The letter provoked fury among non-Catholics. *The Times* sought to puncture Wiseman's pretension by describing him as 'the new-fangled Archbishop of Westminster' whose title signified no more 'than if the Pope had been pleased to confer on the editor of *The Tablet* [a leading Catholic journal] the rank and title of the Duke of Smithfield'. Queen Victoria is said to have been affronted that anyone should claim jurisdiction over a substantial part of her kingdom and the Prime Minister began to talk publicly about 'papal aggression'. Above all, there was a common feeling that to take 'Westminster' as an episcopal title was an insult to the seat of the British government. In 1851 Parliament passed an Ecclesiastical Titles Act, which prohibited the Catholic hierarchy from adopting the names of existing Anglican bishoprics. Nevertheless, these new Roman Catholic dioceses were here to stay. Some nostalgic Catholics might have yearned for more of a sense of continuity with the Middle Ages, but they were to be reminded by the recent convert, John Henry Newman, that they were witnessing a 'second spring' rather than a return to past glories:

> A second temple rises on the ruins of the old. Canterbury has gone its way, and York is gone, and Durham is gone, and Winchester is gone ... but the Church in England has died and the Church lives again. Westminster and Nottingham, Beverley and Hexham, Northampton and Shrewsbury, if the world lasts, shall be names as musical to the ear, as stirring to the heart, as the glories we have lost.

Fanciful as Newman's words might now sound, this was not wishful thinking. This was emphatically the Church *in* England rather than the Church *of* England.

THE NEW CATHOLIC CATHEDRALS

St Chad's, Birmingham

Since the Emancipation Act of 1829 English Catholics had been active in building new churches to cope with increased congregations. A Church which had once flourished only in London, and which had often been succoured in rural areas by a faithful aristocracy, had emerged from its semi-clandestine mission and now had to cope openly with new urban congregations. The Church also had to work against three centuries of ingrained prejudice and suspicion. New churches could not easily be sited in prominent positions, but where Catholics were numerous and where adequate funds were available, large churches were constructed in the anticipation of their being raised to the rank of cathedral. This was notably true of what became St Chad's Cathedral in Birmingham in 1850. St Chad's had been begun on the initiative of Bishop Thomas Walsh, Vicar Apostolic of the Midland District. Walsh was fortunate both in having the active support of the moneyed sixteenth Earl of Shrewsbury and in his choice of architect, the energetic, highly opinionated convert, Augustus Welby Northmore Pugin. Despite his relatively short life, Pugin was to leave an indelible mark both on English Catholicism and on English architecture. In 1839, when work on St Chad's began, he was becoming well known as an architect and as an ardent propagandist for the Gothic style, a style which he insisted should more properly be known as 'Pointed' or, more reverently and succinctly, as 'Christian'. Though firmly persuaded that English medieval architecture was a matter of national pride, Pugin designed St Chad's in red brick (which had scarcely ever been used in England before the sixteenth century) and in a style reminiscent of the great Baltic churches of North Germany. St Chad's needed to be built quickly and economically, and its architect argued that his design and his selected materials were 'appropriate because it is both cheap and effective and Likewise because it is totally different from any *protestant* errection [sic].' The church was completed in just over two years. The site, that of an existing early nineteenth-century Catholic chapel dedicated to

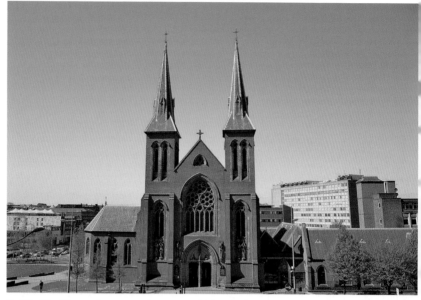

St Chad's, Birmingham, was begun in 1839 to the designs of A.W.N. Pugin, but its surroundings have been radically altered since that time.

St Austin, was a difficult one. The centre of the old 'Gun Quarter' was crammed with workshops and the site sloped away on its eastern side to a canal wharf. As originally conceived, St Chad's was to be an unmistakeably *Catholic* church, one that soared above the low buildings that once hemmed it in. The effect of its symmetrical, twin-spired west façade has now been sadly diminished by the advent in the 1960s of a system of dual carriageways, ring roads and underpasses, the construction of which entailed the destruction of the adjacent Bishop's House (also by Pugin).

The glory of St Chad's, however, is its interior. The cathedral is exceptionally tall, open to its roof timbers which seem almost too delicate, but the resulting impression of spaciousness is splendid. It was once an even more subtly articulate space. A deeply unfortunate re-ordering of the cathedral took place in 1967–8 in which period the great open rood screen, which once separated the recessed choir from the nave, was removed (it now, shorn of its statues, stands in a church in Reading). A further re-ordering in the 1990s has happily undone many of the earlier mistakes and restored a good deal of the

The nave of St Chad's. Pugin's great rood screen, which formerly divided the choir from the nave, was removed in 1967–8.

The new high altar of St Chad's showing (behind) the reliquary of Saint Chad and the reredos, both designed by A.W.N. Pugin.

old colour scheme. The cathedral has always boasted a superb set of fittings, which though sadly depleted in the 1960s, give the church much of its distinctive beauty. The relics of St Chad (rescued from Lichfield Cathedral at the time of the Reformation) are enshrined in a gilded reliquary above the high altar and the altar itself is decked with six silver-plated candlesticks designed by Pugin in 1854. Pugin was also responsible for the monument to Bishop Walsh (finished in 1850 and exhibited in the Gothic Court of the Crystal Palace in 1851) and for the Lady Chapel altar and screens (1841). The architect, who travelled widely collecting antique church art, managed to acquire the Netherlandish oak choir stalls of *c*.1520. It was he who prompted Lord Shrewsbury to give the beautiful hexagonal medieval nave pulpit, which it is claimed came from the Abbey of St Gertrude in Louvain. St Chad's was solemnly consecrated in June 1841 with the architect acting as master of ceremonies and with thirteen bishops in attendance. The liturgical celebrations, which extended over five days, included a vast procession through the streets of Birmingham accompanying the translation of the relics of the titular saint.

St Chad's at Birmingham, approaches Pugin's *beau idéal* of a large church, one whose interior glows with colour and imagery and in which due Catholic ceremonial could be fittingly observed. Only one other of Pugin's churches – that at Cheadle in Staffordshire – properly fulfils that ambition, but Cheadle was lavishly designed as a parish church, not as a prospective cathedral. Pugin's other significant English Catholic cathedrals, those at Newcastle, Nottingham and Southwark, have far less of the flair, brilliance and serenity of St Chad's. St Mary's at Newcastle-upon-Tyne was finished in 1844 and became the cathedral of the Bishop of Hexham in 1850 (the see was renamed 'Hexham and Newcastle' in 1861). It is in the Decorated style and is fortunate to have a prominent position close to Newcastle's superb Classical railway station. The tall, well-proportioned, stone spire, which Pugin had always hoped to add to his church, was not in fact constructed until 1872 (to the designs of A.M. Dunn and E.J. Hansom). Despite it substance, St Mary's has more of the air of a large parish church than a cathedral. Its interior is relatively plain and was rendered even plainer by a re-ordering in the 1980s which removed the choir screen and re-coloured the walls in an unbecoming insipid shade. Fortunately, a redecoration in the late 1990s has brought back a bolder colour scheme. Pugin's stone reredos, font and pulpit survive. What makes St Mary's most memorable, however, is the glowing stained glass in the large traceried window in the choir, and in the two windows at the east end of the side aisles. All three were designed by Pugin and made in 1844 by William Wailes of Newcastle.

NOTTINGHAM CATHEDRAL

Writing in 1841 Pugin hoped that when it was complete St Barnabas at Nottingham would be 'the most perfect revival of a large parish church that has yet been accomplished ... and to the minutest details this church will be a strict revival of Catholic antiquity.' St Barnabas was built at the request of Fr Robert Willson, who selected both the site and the dedication but who left for Australia to become the first Bishop of Hobart, before the church was fully completed. Willson was consecrated at St Chad's at Birmingham arrayed in a magnificent set of vestments provided by Pugin. It was Willson, a pioneer colonial bishop and penal reformer, who persuaded the overworked Pugin to provide designs for churches, church fittings and vestments in his distant new see. Nottingham Cathedral, as the church of St Barnabas became in 1850, showed its ambition from the first. It was built between 1841 and 1844, and when consecrated it was, for a short time, the largest Catholic parish church in England. With the help of funds provided by the ever-munificent Lord Shrewsbury, Pugin built a cruciform stone church in the Early English style with details derived from local medieval precedents (notably the ruined Cistercian Abbey at Croxden in Staffordshire, which had been founded by one of Shrewsbury's ancestors). The crossing is crowned with a handsome tower and spire and the cathedral ensemble includes a clergy house and a former convent (now converted into flats). Unfortunately, the interior retains little that speaks of Pugin's decorative genius. The rood screen, rood and high altar were removed in the late nineteenth century, many of Pugin's stained-glass windows were replaced, and another drastic re-ordering in 1961–2 did further damage. St Barnabas, lit by lancet windows, was always a dark church but the interior of the cathedral was painted white in 1993. The only relief from this uniform whiteness is provided by the Blessed Sacrament Chapel, originally designed by Pugin but beautifully and imaginatively redecorated by J. Alphege Pippet in 1933. Bishop Willson, having resigned from his Tasmanian see, died in Nottingham in 1866 and is buried in the cathedral's crypt. A particularly refined gilt-wood crucifix, designed for him by Pugin in 1847, stands on a nearby altar.

St George's, Southwark

The site of St George's Cathedral in Southwark was purchased from the City of London in 1839 and a substantial church was constructed to Pugin's designs in 1840–8. The dedication derived from the site, 'St George's Fields' having once been open land in the ancient parish of St George in the Borough. Ironically, it was in this open space that the deranged Lord George Gordon addressed a large crowd of anti-Catholic demonstrators in 1780 in the prelude to what became known as the Gordon Riots. Some commentators have even claimed that Gordon harangued his followers from the spot where the present high altar stands. The cathedral's siting remains prominent but what should have distinguished it both from a distance and head-on was the great west tower and spire proposed by Pugin. The tower remains stumpily and awkwardly incomplete and, despite several unrealized plans and fresh designs, the spire has, alas, never been built. St George's, designed to accommodate 3,000 worshippers, was consecrated with a Pontifical High Mass on 4 July 1848 in the presence of fourteen English and European bishops (dramatically enough, the Archbishop of Paris, who was due to attend, had died shortly before from wounds received on the barricades during the 1848 Revolution). To the English press the ceremonial consecration marked a revolution in itself. Although *The Times* rudely remarked on 'the number of ugly faces' in the clergy procession, *The Standard* commented that since the reign of Queen Mary there had been:

'no such remarkable day in London for the Roman Catholics ... For the first time since 1558 there was seen clustered together in the immediate neighbourhood of the Archbishop of Canterbury [i.e. the nearby Lambeth Palace], foreign bishops, some three hundred priests, monks in their white gowns and hoods, friars of various orders, and all wearing rich robes or poor habiliments indicative either of the high rank to which they had attained in their church, or the poverty to which they had devoted themselves.'

A similar pomp was observed when Cardinal Nicholas Wiseman was enthroned as Archbishop of Westminster here on 6 December 1850 (appropriately enough, the feast-day of St Nicholas). It was a singularly foggy day and little light filtered through the cathedral's stained glass. The gloom of London's largest and grandest Catholic

On 16 April 1941 an incendiary bomb set fire to the roof of St George's and within minutes the cathedral was ablaze. Here Archbishop Amigo surveys the damage, with the ruined nave of Pugin clearly visible.

church was, however, brightened by the cardinal's scarlet robes and by a silk and gold canopy carried over his head by a group o eminent recent converts to Catholicism. The first Archbishop o Westminster was formally inducted to his new jurisdiction to the strains of a Haydn Mass.

The finished St George's Cathedral pleased few of Pugin's contem poraries. The architect himself complained of a severe lack of funds which had crippled his ambitious plans, but it was a sarcastic foot note in John Ruskin's influential *The Stones of Venice* that served to deflate any pretension to grandeur that the new cathedral might have claimed. We can judge Pugin's achievement now only from drawings and photographs, for in April 1941 an incendiary bomb lodged itself in St George's timber roof and the cathedral was rapidly burnt out What survived were the walls of the outer aisles and the shell of the choir. The moulded stone piers that formerly supported the open timber roof were calcified and proved beyond repair.

The diocese was inspired enough to employ the architect Romilly Craze for the cathedral's restoration in the years 1953–8. Craze did much more than 'restore' the ruined cathedral; he virtually created a new one in an expressive, distinctly twentieth-century Gothic style. The new piers, which were intended to support a vault, give an impression of substance to a broad nave that rises to a clerestory lit by large windows with free Gothic tracery. Above the surviving aisles Craze introduced ingenious flying ribs in the manner of those at Bristol Cathedral. Pugin's legacy can still, however, be glimpsed in the severely re-ordered choir (though its great eastern window is now filled with over-bright modern glass), in the chantry chapel of the Petre family, in the fittings of the Blessed Sacrament Chapel, and in the broken fragments of the old high altar preserved in a side chapel. A rectangular box of a Lady Chapel with tall, flat-topped windows was added on the north side 1961–3.

Pugin's intimate associations with St George's continued into the last phase of his short life. He married his third wife, Jane Knill, there in August 1848. It was the first marriage celebrated in the church. The delicately vaulted Knill family chantry, designed by Pugin's son in 1856, and built in memory of Jane's relatives, survives in the south aisle. Unhappily, it was Jane who had to tend to her new husband during his breakdown in 1852. At midsummer he stayed briefly with his friend, the faithful builder George Myers, in a house opposite the cathedral. From there he was admitted to the nearby Bethlem Hospital (the building now houses the Imperial War Museum). Aged only forty, Pugin died at his home in Ramsgate in September 1852. Variable though his work may be, no medieval architect could have boasted of having been responsible for the construction of four English cathedrals. Despite the man-made disasters that have befallen those cathedrals, there is ample surviving evidence to suggest quite how extraordinary Pugin's contribution to the revival of Catholicism in England is.

COMPROMISE AND TRIUMPH

SALFORD CATHEDRAL

The Cathedral of St John the Evangelist at Salford is a substantial Gothic building of 1844–8 that replaced an earlier chapel. Pugin had produced a design for the church in 1842 but withdrew from the commission. He was replaced by Matthew Hadfield who drew, ably enough, on the medieval precedents of the large churches at Newark in Nottinghamshire, and Howden and Selby in Yorkshire. It is a stone cruciform church with a tower over its crossing crowned with a tall stone spire modelled on that of Newark. Salford Cathedral is, therefore, very self-consciously *unlike* Manchester's Anglican cathedral which is less than a mile away on the other side of the River Irwell. Its interior is a dignified interpretation of fourteenth-century Decorated precedents with some richly carved details in the former choir (which now serves as a Lady Chapel). Following an over-rigorous application of the decrees of the Second Vatican Council, Salford Cathedral suffered drastically. Between 1972 and 1983 the old high altar was destroyed and its elaborate reredos reduced in size to be replaced by a free-standing altar at the crossing. The sanctuary was either stripped or mutilated, most of the side altars removed and the walls and stonework were rendered in a nondescript, and inappropriately puritanical, white and magnolia. There is now an unobstructed view of the large and elegant East Window with its glass by William Wailes of 1856. Apart from this wonderful window, the only recall of the cathedral's former rich colour scheme is to be found in the Blessed Sacrament Chapel, designed in 1884 by another of Pugin's sons, Peter Paul. The chapel contains the relics of St Aurelius (acquired in Rome by Cardinal Vaughan). A wonderfully expressive, and notably realistic recumbent effigy of the saint is placed under the altar.

NORTHAMPTON, SHREWSBURY AND PLYMOUTH CATHEDRALS

In 1850 the new Bishops of Liverpool, Beverley, Northampton, Shrewsbury and Plymouth had no cathedral churches comparable to those of their brother bishops. Liverpool had great ambitions for a cathedral worthy of a populous city with a strong Catholic identity, but those ambitions took well over a century to be finally realized. The diocese of Beverley, which was already essentially based in Leeds, was formally divided into two new sees in 1878, with bishops in Leeds and Middlesbrough. The cathedrals of both, like Liverpool's, now date from the twentieth century. The first Bishop of Northampton, with a diocese originally stretching from the Midlands into East Anglia, designated the collegiate chapel of St Felix, built by Pugin in 1844, as his cathedral. Twenty years later a new aisled nave was added to the church by Edward Pugin. This structure was in turn demolished in 1955 when the church was extended to the east and the sanctuary moved to the old west end. It was re-ordered yet again in 1998. Not unexpectedly, therefore, Northampton Cathedral remains something of an architectural compromise. Bishop James Brown of Shrewsbury, most of whose diocese included the north of Wales, was consecrated at St George's Southwark in 1850. He had as yet no cathedral of his own. The ever-generous Earl of Shrewsbury acquired land and offered to finance a new church designed by the overworked Pugin, but the deaths of both the architect and the sixteenth Earl meant that plans had to put on hold. It was Pugin's son, Edward who oversaw the construction of Shrewsbury's modest, but tall, cathedral in the years

1853–6 (it was the new patron, the young seventeenth Earl, Bertram, who chose the church's dedication to 'Our Lady Help of Christians and St Peter of Alcantara'). Sadly, Bertram died before the new cathedral was dedicated, though his mother gave the church's font in memory of him. Structurally, little has changed since 1856 but fittings have been moved or disposed of. The pulpit, altar, reredos and altar-rails have gone, as has any trace of painted or stencilled wall decoration. The cathedral does, however, retain some striking woodwork (notably the wonderfully florid rood of 1885 and the gilded tabernacle in what was St Winefride's Chapel). Its most memorable feature is the collection of distinctive 1920s stained glass in the aisles and the chancel designed by the nun, Margaret Rope.

The first Bishop of Plymouth was only able to take possession of his cathedral, designed by the Catholic architect brothers, Joseph Aloysius and Charles Francis Hansom, in 1858. It is situated on rising ground in the north-western inner suburbs of the city and survived the heavy bombing of Plymouth in the 1940s relatively unscathed. In 1866 its most distinctive feature, a thin 205-foot spire, was added to its north-west tower. The cathedral was ably restored in the early 1920s by F.A. Walters, but further works in 1956–7, and the inevitable post-Vatican 2 re-ordering in the 1970s, have rendered the already sparse interior essentially a twentieth-century creation.

WESTMINSTER CATHEDRAL

Although Cardinal Wiseman, Archbishop of Westminster, had initially opposed the division of the old London District into two separate Catholic sees (one to the north of the Thames and one to the south), by 1850 he had accepted that his jurisdiction did not stretch into that of the new bishop of Southwark. He had been enthroned with great pomp in his neighbour's large cathedral church, but Wiseman was content to name the less commodious, but historically resonant, St Mary Moorfields, north of the City of London, as his pro-cathedral. When he died in 1865 there were still no firm plans to find either a site or an architect for a new church.

His successor, the imperious ex-Anglican, Cardinal Henry Edward Manning, somewhat dispassionately supported the idea of building a cathedral in Westminster in memory of Wiseman. A strip of land was acquired in 1867 and a commission was given to Henry Clutton (a fellow convert) to design an elaborate church in the Gothic style. Indecision hampered progress and other financial demands took precedence over the luxury of a cathedral. Adjacent sites were acquired and plans changed and then changed yet again. In the end Clutton had been obliged to produce no fewer than four designs, the last being for a cathedral in an English style but with a distinctly French ground plan. What Clutton proposed was a substantial church on the scale of the newly completed medieval cathedral at Cologne, but by now the diocese's resources stretched neither to starting work nor to envisaging a long-term commitment to a costly sculptural and decorative scheme. Clutton's designs had been effectively abandoned. In 1884, with the prospect of generous funding and another (this time Austrian) architect on offer, Manning disposed of the original building plot and bought another. This was the eight-acre site of the former Tothill Fields Prison, close to the newly established thoroughfare of Victoria Street. By the time Manning died in 1892, however, neither the proposed Austrian architect nor the funding was still available.

It was the third Archbishop of Westminster, Herbert Vaughan, who was acutely aware that substantive work on a new cathedral had to be started during his episcopate. Vaughan also recognized that a Gothic-style cathedral was no longer feasible. The Victorian Gothic Revival was far from dead – indeed, it was in its last glorious flowering – but if the new cathedral were to be of stone the costs of its construction and decoration would be prohibitive. There were other pressing reasons for the rejection of the Gothic style. It was argued that the new metropolitan cathedral should not be seen as a modern architectural rival to Westminster Abbey (which we should remember had itself briefly served as a cathedral). Initially, Vaughan aspired to construct a spacious basilica on the Early Christian model, something akin to the lost Old St Peter's in Rome or to St Paul's Outside the Walls (which had been rebuilt after a disastrous fire and re-dedicated only thirty-seven years before). Medieval cathedrals in Europe had generally had a cruciform plan, with the choir divided from the nave by a solid screen. This was particularly true of the former monastic cathedrals of England where the monks' part of the church was clearly separate from areas open to public worship. Pugin and his followers were so wedded to medieval precedent that a cathedral without a clear division between the laity and the priestly celebrants of worship seemed almost heretical. Cardinal Vaughan, who was naturally more familiar with the great churches of Rome than with the ancient English cathedrals, knew that a return to a pre-medieval basilican plan would offer large numbers of worshippers a clear view of the altar, unimpeded either by a solid or an open screen. But he was a practical rather than a radical thinker about church architecture. The Roman basilicas had consisted of a tall, open-columned nave, flanked by two or four aisles, and with a raised semi-circular apse at the east end. Liturgical processions could move freely and ceremonially from the nave to the altar through a space unbroken by a conspicuous towered crossing or by transepts. What may also have been in Vaughan's mind was that a large basilican church could also provide a sacred auditorium for the delivery of long public sermons (late nineteenth-century Catholics, like their Protestant contemporaries, held gifted preachers in high esteem).

Vaughan appointed as his architect John Francis Bentley, a Catholic convert and a man of genius. The architectural brief shifted rapidly from an Early Christian style, to which Bentley was opposed, to the Byzantine, a style to which both client and architect responded. This decision also carried the implication that the cathedral could be constructed quickly in brick and, once it was open for worship, its decoration in mosaic could steadily follow over an extended period. Bentley was consequently dispatched to Italy to study precedents. There had been a purposeful revival in interest in Byzantium and in Byzantine art in the latter years of the nineteenth century. John Ruskin had consistently adulated the wonders of the Basilica of St Mark at Venice, lovingly delineating the colours of its marbles and the richness of its mosaics, but the serious study of the ancient churches at Milan, Ravenna and Constantinople was relatively new. Bentley got to know Italian models well but his only

The nave of J.F. Bentley's Westminster Cathedral was completed in 1902. Supported on eight yellow Verona marble columns, the baldacchino over the high altar was added in 1906. It was Bentley's last design for the cathedral.

intimate acquaintance with the greatest of all Byzantine churches, Hagia Sophia at Constantinople, came through meticulously illustrated architectural books and photographs. When he returned from his European journey in the spring of 1895, the architect was well aware of the complexity of the task confronting him. Although he had been trained in the Gothic school, and had built some remarkable parish churches in the style (notably the church of the Holy Rood at Watford), he had now been obliged to learn a new architectural language. More awkwardly, he must have been acutely aware that most of the greatest surviving examples of the larger Byzantine churches were not in the shape of an ancient Roman Basilica, indeed the sheer wonder of Hagia Sophia lay in the fact that it was a great, solid, square-shaped space which supported a single saucer dome. If Bentley wanted to add an attached bell tower to his design there were again very few useful precedents in the strictly Byzantine style. What may also have made the brief more complicated was the fact that those churches still dedicated to the Eastern Orthodox rite would have had a great iconostasis, or icon screen, as a dominant decorative feature, blocking off a small chancel space from a much

164

larger congregational area. Nevertheless, Bentley responded to his commission with admirable dexterity and enthusiasm. His third and final plan for the new cathedral was ready by the early summer of 1895 and work began on the new foundations in July. 'He wished to build two campaniles,' Vaughan wrote, 'I said one would be enough for me. For the rest he had a free hand.'

Westminster Cathedral was, and is, a radical departure from conventional assumptions about what a 'traditional' cathedral should look like. It is oblong in shape, three hundred and sixty feet long and a one hundred and fifty six feet wide. Its massive exterior is highly distinctive. A high plinth of glinting Welsh granite is surmounted by alternate layers of fine red bricks relieved with bands of white Portland stone. The long nave carries three concrete saucer domes while a fourth dome, pierced with windows, in the manner of Hagia Sophia, crowns the sanctuary. The choir sing from a raised apse behind the altar (Vaughan had originally hoped that Benedictine monks might chant the Divine Liturgy on a daily basis, but this was not to be). The church is lit by round-headed windows, set with clear glass roundels in a variety of patterns. Stained glass, which was deemed inappropriate by Bentley, is notable for its absence. The rich colours of the interior derive instead from the superb monolithic marble columns with their white capitals and from the exotic marble panels that now sheath the brick piers of the nave. Bentley referred to this sheathing and to the prospect of mosaics rising above it as a 'veneering' of his building. Although the intended mosaic decoration of the upper areas of the cathedral has still not been realized, the exposed brickwork serves to emphasize both the severity of the structure and a sense of sombre mystery. The mosaics in the side chapels are now largely complete and these glow with a surprising variety of figurative and vegetal decoration, ranging in style from the neo-Byzantine and the neo-Norman to the distinctly less-referential styles of the early twenty-first century. The Lady Chapel at the east end of the south aisle of the cathedral (completed 1932) offers a foretaste in miniature of what the finished church might look like, but it is the Arts-and-Crafts Chapel of St Andrew of 1910–16 which is in every sense the most aesthetically satisfying, combining exquisite detailing with first-rate craftsmanship. The most striking feature of the cathedral is the noble baldacchino in the raised sanctuary. It was completed only in 1906 to Bentley's design and consists of an inlaid white marble canopy supported on eight superb yellow Verona marble columns.

Bentley's designs for the sanctuary were his last work for the cathedral. Though he was able to walk through the completed shell of his masterpiece the day before he died in March 1902, he was never able to witness either its completion or its consecration. The godfather of the great project, Cardinal Vaughan, died in the following June. The first Mass was sung in the Cathedral in 1903, the year that also saw the first London performance of Elgar's oratorio *The Dream of Gerontius* in its bare domed spaces. The cathedral was finally consecrated on 28 June 1910, with the fourth archbishop of Westminster, Francis Bourne, officiating. Generally, Westminster Cathedral has been singularly fortunate in the quality of the fittings that have been added since Bentley's time and in the fact that no major re-ordering has marred its integrity. The fourteen Hopton Wood stone panels of the Stations of the Cross on the west faces of the piers of the nave (1913–18) are especially remarkable. There was no Byzantine precedent for such objects of Catholic devotion and Bentley left no sketches, let alone designs, for them. It was Cardinal Bourne, who insisted that the chosen artist be a Catholic, who selected Eric Gill for the commission (though Gill had only recently been received into the Church). It was an inspired choice, though Bourne probably never guessed *how* inspired. 'I can only work in one style,' Gill told a newspaper in 1915, 'and that is my own.' The sculptures have something of the starkness of Romanesque carving but they are also unmistakeably both 'modern' and astylar. Gill's beautiful lettering of the explicatory Latin and English texts (now coloured in red) boldly complements the strangely eloquent stiffness of the figures. These sculpted panels, Gill memorably claimed were 'a statement without adjectives'.

Even in its incomplete state Westminster Cathedral can properly be claimed to be the finest English church of the nineteenth century. It is certainly the most daringly innovative English cathedral of the age that produced it. Having escaped major damage in the Second World War, and having endured the wholesale reconstruction of

The thirteenth Station of the Cross designed and carved by Eric Gill for Westminster Cathedral (1913–18).

Victoria Street in the 1960s and 1970s, it now stands exposed to Victoria Street in its own small piazza. Its thin red-brick campanile may no longer dominate the London skyline, but it has a unique claim to celebrity. It is the only cathedral tower to figure dramatically in an Alfred Hitchcock film (*Foreign Correspondent* of 1940). Westminster Cathedral has received two popes and functioned flexibly at the centre of English Catholic life for over a century. Its ceremony and its daily round of choral liturgical worship has a world-wide reputation and yet it attracts and moves the simplest and most silent of prayerful visitors. It remains a model of what a great cathedral can be in the modern age.

6

THE TWENTIETH-CENTURY CATHEDRAL

LIVERPOOL'S ANGLICAN CATHEDRAL

IN THE YEAR 1900 Liverpool was a flourishing world-class city. In 1881, a year after it had been raised to city status, it had a population of some 611,000. By 1907 it is estimated that its population had risen to nearly 747,000. It was the second largest seaport of the United Kingdom and it was the main port of communication with the United States and Canada. It had civic and commercial architecture that was admired on both sides of the Atlantic. It had been the see of a Roman Catholic bishop since 1850 and of an Anglican one since 1880, but neither bishop had a cathedral worthy of the name. A volume of the *Bell's Cathedral* Series, which offered an itinerary of all the English cathedrals for American visitors landing in the port, passed over Liverpool's in a dismissive sentence.

Since 1880 the Anglican bishop had made do with the late-seventeenth-century parish church of St Peter. It was a galleried, Classical, oblong box in Church Street, hemmed in by commercial buildings. Having become redundant both as a cathedral and as a parish church, it was finally demolished in 1922. In 1885 an Act of Parliament authorized the diocese to begin work on a new cathedral on the site of the now vanished St John's Church near St George's Hall. A competition was won by Sir William Emerson who produced a strange hotch-potch of a design for a domed Gothic cathedral which would have looked cramped on its confined site and, moreover, would have clashed horribly with the great Classical bulk of St George's Hall. Although preliminary work was begun on this new church the project had happily lapsed by 1888. It was the second Bishop of Liverpool, Francis James Chavasse, who moved matters forward in 1901. A spectacularly fine new site for a cathedral was acquired on rising land at St James's Mount, overlooking a former stone quarry that had been developed in the 1820s as the romantic chasm that is St James's Cemetery. Bishop Chavasse began a campaign to raise the level of local enthusiasm and funds for his plans. In June he told a meeting in Liverpool Town Hall that since the Reformation the Church of England had built only one new cathedral and that was in 'the remote and poor diocese of Truro'. He went on to insist that the 'great commercial city of Liverpool' was the centre of a see four times the size of Truro and merited a finer building for three leading reasons. Firstly, it would bear visible

The Anglican Cathedral at Liverpool was designed by Giles Gilbert Scott in the nineteenth century. The tower, emended from Scott's original concept, was finally completed in 1942.

witness for God 'in the midst of the great city' and speak for the Divine just as St George's Hall spoke for the municipality. Secondly, the large church was needed for 'diocesan and popular services'. Thirdly, it would serve to 'express and deepen the spiritual longings and aspirations of many among us'. Chavasse's definition of what an urban cathedral should be in the twentieth century is revealing. Gone is the idea of another secluded, predominantly rural-based, provincial 'Barchester'. Gone, too, is the idea of a bishop's church which would be run for the benefit of its clergy rather than its lay congregations. What Chavasse wanted, therefore, was a great church for the people of a great city. It would express not the power of the Church, but the *presence* of the Church. Dynamic, commercial, populous, architecturally proud, Liverpool needed both an assertive statement about God and a statement about itself.

Bishop Chavasse's dream was to be given real substance during his episcopate (he resigned from his see in 1923). In 1903 a two-stage competition was held to find an architect. There were 103 applicants, of whom five were shortlisted. Interestingly, there was no insistence on the new cathedral being in the Gothic style and among the designs submitted was one in the Byzantine style and one in the Classical. The winning architect was a young man of twenty-two, the Catholic grandson of George Gilbert Scott, Giles. Giles Scott's design was for a strikingly innovative cruciform Gothic church. Some members of the advisory committee expressed reservations about Scott's Catholicism (no small issue in sectarian Liverpool at the time), others protested about his youth and inexperience, but the two eminent assessors of the competition were insistent that it was Scott they wanted. However, a condition was imposed on the young architect that he should collaborate with one of those assessors, the greatest master of the late-Victorian Gothic, G.F. Bodley. It was not an easy collaboration and the arrangement was terminated when Bodley died in 1907.

The influence of Bodley's superbly refined late-Gothic style is evident in the first part of Liverpool Cathedral to be completed: its delicately vaulted Lady Chapel. Work had begun on the cathedral in 1904 (the foundation stone was laid by Edward VII) and it took a further six years to complete the chapel that could be used for worship while work continued on the main body of the church. Because of the lie of the ground, the floor level of the Lady Chapel is below that of the cathedral's choir which would eventually rise beside it. It is still something of a detached space, cathedralesque in its magnificent proportions, but somehow like a mini-cathedral beyond the great cathedral. Bishop Chavasse, who consecrated the Lady Chapel in June 1910, approved Scott's revised plans for the remaining body of the cathedral in the same year. In effect, Scott had completely redesigned the original proposal, dispensing with the proposed twin towers over the transepts and replacing them with a massive central tower. The ground plan changed, too, with the grand area under the new tower, which Scott referred to as his 'Central Square', now serving as an extension of the nave and providing an impressive congregational space. The architect conceived of a long building programme stretching over some seventy years. He continued to revise his plans until his death in 1960, but the completed cathedral was not to be formally opened for another eighteen years after that.

Work on the Liverpool's huge choir was to continue during the First World War and it was not ready for consecration until July 1924. The choir is lit by a vast window in the English Decorated style, but the great stone reredos that rises underneath it has an unmistakeable Spanish feel (it is derived from the entrance portal of the College of San Gregorio at Valladolid). Scott had travelled extensively in Spain soon after construction at Liverpool had begun. The distinctive Spanish accent to Scott's Gothic is pervasive, but it is the very weight of the architectural elements that make Liverpool Cathedral so memorable. Scott's splendid bridge that divides his choir from the nave owes a debt to the interior of Santo Tomas at Avila but, as elsewhere in the design, such influences are transformed and moulded into an hugely novel, and sometimes breathtaking unity. Despite bomb damage in the Second World War (when most of the pre-war glass was blown out) work on the tower and the transepts beneath continued apace. The 331-foot tower was completed in 1942 and the bridge beneath it in 1949. Work continued on the nave until 1978. In order to bring the prospect of completion forward, and to cut down on soaring costs, Scott had already reduced this nave to three bays. It was far from finished when he died and a simplified compromise of a design for the nave and the West Front was agreed upon in 1968. The cathedral was finally declared 'finished' in 1978.

Liverpool's Anglican Cathedral is remarkable not so much for its detail or its interior fittings as for its surprisingly elegant bulk. Despite the truncation of Scott's nave it is the sheer grandeur of his concept that still leaves a lasting impression. Seen from below, looking up from St James's Cemetery it has the kind of theatricality that we can properly call 'Romantic'. Like one of the great medieval cathedrals the huge, subtly chamfered tower dominates its exterior, but, unlike a medieval cathedral, Liverpool's interiors are unbroken hall-like spaces, unimpeded by columns, screens and distracting ornament. Seen too, as it was once meant to be, by travellers arriving by sea from the USA, Liverpool Cathedral makes its presence felt as a single monolith as opposed to the clustered towers of New York. Even for seafarers coming from Ireland or for holidaymakers returning from the Isle of Man the cathedral dominates the city as ships move up the Mersey. The tower is a stump seen from a distance, but as the traveller draws nearer, the tower and the great church below are revealed: the effect is extraordinary. No other cathedral, old or new, seems so spellbinding because so few are seen from the water. If only the dome of Lutyens' Catholic Cathedral had been built to complement it, Liverpool's skyline would have no rival in the world.

LIVERPOOL'S METROPOLITAN CATHEDRAL

The story of the Metropolitan Cathedral of Christ the King, as the Catholic cathedral is properly known, is radically different from that of the city's Anglican cathedral. The first Catholic bishops of Liverpool used the church of St Nicholas in Hawke Street as their pro-cathedral. A far grander building was begun in Everton in 1856 to the designs of Edward Pugin, but only the eastern chapels were actually built and these were relegated to serving merely as the parish church of Our Lady Immaculate until they were demolished in the 1980s. St Nicholas was also demolished (the fate of so many of Liverpool's older inner-city churches) in 1972. In 1911 the Holy See divided what had been the single English province of Westminster into three, with two new archbishops, serving the Midlands and the North, in Birmingham and Liverpool. Although the new archbishops of Liverpool clearly merited a cathedral worthy of their dignity as metropolitans, it was not until Archbishop Richard Downey was appointed in 1928 that positive steps were taken to initiate an especially grand project. Downey bought the site of a former workhouse at the top of Mount Pleasant and Brownlow Hill and resolved to build 'a cathedral for our time'. A great church on this raised site would make an assertive statement as bold as that of the Anglican cathedral half a mile away. Downey wanted something distinctive and non-Gothic and subsequently appointed Sir Edwin Lutyens as his architect. It was a very personal decision. There was no distraction of a competition, and, self-evidently great architect though he was, Lutyens was conspicuously *not* a Catholic. Liverpool Metropolitan Cathedral would therefore be the first Catholic cathedral in England since the restoration of the hierarchy not to be designed by a Catholic architect. What Lutyens designed in 1932 would have been one of the largest cathedrals in the world: 680 feet long, 400 feet wide, and with a stupendous dome 168 feet in diameter rising to a height of 510 feet (larger than that of St Peter's in Rome). This megalomaniac project seemed feasible at the time and the Pope himself had given his approval to the designs following a meeting with the architect in Rome. Its dimensions can still be traced in the surviving granite crypt and appreciated even more in Lutyens's drawings and in the superb model that he exhibited at the Royal Academy in 1934 (the damaged model is now in the Walker Art Gallery). A foundation stone had been laid in June 1933 and work on the foundations and the crypt went ahead until they ceased abruptly in 1941. Having been used as air-raid shelters during the Second World War, work on the building slowly resumed in the mid-1950s. It was only when it became obvious that the original estimate of a £3 million was too low, and that the domed cathedral would in fact cost in the region of £27 million, that the project was sadly abandoned in 1959.

It was not just that financial circumstances had radically

The Metropolitan Cathedral at Liverpool was built 1962–7. The steps leading up to the raised podium on which the cathedral stands were added in 2003.

changed by 1959, so too had received opinions on architecture and liturgy. Archbishop Heenan who commissioned Frederick Gibberd (another non-Catholic) to design a substitute cathedral in the starkly Modernist mode, was also determined that it should emphatically be a church that would 'enshrine the altar of sacrifice'. Gibberd's cathedral of 1962–7 has a circular plan with the altar at the very centre of it. Although there were existing precedents for this plan in post-war parish churches and in the new cathedral in Brasilia, Gibberd's design was both radical and strikingly impressive. Lutyens's crypt had to be incorporated and this Gibberd achieved by using its roof as a rectangular plaza from the end of which the new building could rise. And rise it does. Critics have described it as a kind of concrete tepee, or wigwam, but it is far more properly a buttressed corona with a high lantern crowned with pinnacles. This determining feature not only recalls a Crown of Thorns but, more potently, the triumphant theological assertion of the cathedral's dedication: 'Christ the King'. It also has distinct echoes of Alan of Walsingham's equally daring

174

fourteenth-century lantern at Ely Cathedral, though at Liverpool the lantern is isolated and entire of itself.

The interior of the cathedral is just as successful. Archbishop Heenan's insistence on a central altar was realized with memorable theatricality. Above the altar is a suspended canopy of aluminium rods. Another crown, of course, but it has the unmistakeable look of a lighting rig (which it actually is). In daylight hours much of the cathedral's bluish light streams down from the cylindrical lantern tower, its large windows filled by abstract glass by John Piper and Patrick Reyntiens. At ground level concentric curved benches radiate out from the altar on a grey and white marble floor.

Significant structural repairs in the 1990s have altered important aspects of Liverpool cathedral's exterior. The concrete framework, which was originally clad with the kind of white mosaic popular with Modernist architects, is now coated in glass-reinforced plastic of dreary grey colour and the plaza is paved in concrete flags rather than with slate. The interior of the cathedral maintains its mystery but it has, alas, been cluttered with awkwardly conventional and often unworthy fittings.

The light-filled interior of Liverpool Metropolitan Cathedral showing above the centrally planned altar the baldacchino as a crown-like canopy of aluminium rods supporting lights and loudspeakers.

BIRMINGHAM CATHEDRAL

Birmingham is not Liverpool, nor would it ever claim to be
Nineteenth-century Liverpool aspired to assert its cultural eminence with very good architecture. Birmingham did not. When an
Anglican see of Birmingham was established in 1905 the city could
already claim to be the second city of England, but its Anglican
bishops have been content to use the city's parish church of St
Philip as their cathedral. That said, St Philip's is one of the finest
early eighteenth-century churches in England and, small as it is, it
serves well enough as a cathedral. Its architect, Thomas Archer, was
a Warwickshire man well aware of the Baroque architecture of contemporary Italy. The galleried St Philip's was built in 1710–15 on the
edge of what was then the rapidly expanding town of Birmingham.
It, and its landscaped churchyard, lie now at the very centre of the
city of Birmingham. The elegant lead-domed tower was completed
in 1725, and in 1883 Archer's original apse was extended eastwards
and the windows of this new choir were filled with the cathedral's

St Philip's Cathedral in Birmingham was built 1710–25. The choir was rebuilt and
extended in the late nineteenth century.

The stained glass in the west window of St Philip's Cathedral, Birmingham, showing the Last Judgment, was designed by Edward Burne-Jones in 1897 and made by Morris & Co.

outstanding feature – the glorious stained-glass windows designed by Sir Edward Burne-Jones (who had been born in Birmingham). The eyes of any visitor to St Philip's are drawn inexorably to its richly columned east end and to Burne-Jones's windows showing the Nativity, the Ascension and the Crucifixion. The finest of Burne-Jones's glass is, however, that found in the west window (1897) representing the Last Judgment with red-clothed angels draped around a white-clad Christ.

SOUTHWARK CATHEDRAL

In the same year that the diocese of Birmingham was created, the parish church of St Saviour in Southwark became the cathedral church of the new diocese of Southwark in London. The architectural history of the church is almost as complicated as that of the new see. In the Middle Ages the area south of the River Thames had been part of the large diocese of Winchester. The bishops of

Southwark Cathedral from the east, showing the surviving chapels. Here stood the chapels of St Mary Magdalene (demolished in 1822) and the Bishop's Chapel (pulled down in 1830 to improve access to the new London Bridge).

Winchester had a palace on Bankside and the fragmentary remains of the palace's Great Hall lie close to the present cathedral. One of the most eminent of the bishops of Winchester, the articulate Lancelot Andrewes, was buried in a tomb in St Saviour's in 1626. In 1877 south London became part of the much-expanded diocese of Rochester, only to be separated from it again in 1905 when Bishop Edward Talbot translated from Rochester to take charge of the new see of Southwark. The present cathedral's dedication, 'St Saviour and St Mary Overie', tells us of the church's tangled history. It was founded as an Augustinian priory church dedicated to St Mary in 1106 (the term 'Overie' means 'over the river'). At the Dissolution in 1539 the church was rededicated as St Saviour's and became the parish church of the northern part of the borough. The fact that since 1905 it has been known simply as 'Southwark Cathedral' suggests the ease with which it assumed its new dignity.

The church stands prominently on the south side of London Bridge. As such it had long imprinted itself on London's identity. From its tower Wenceslas Hollar drew his much-reproduced views of the City of London and Bankside in the early seventeenth century and the church appears in most historic views of the metropolis taken from the south. Its eastern arm had been rebuilt in a particularly refined style in the early thirteenth century, and a great stone reredos erected behind the high altar in 1528, but from the time of the Reformation the church suffered a series of degradations. Having escaped the Great Fire of London in 1666 it remained, with Westminster Abbey, the most substantial medieval church in central London but, unlike its royal neighbour, its three centuries as a parish church meant that it suffered at the hands of largely indifferent churchwardens. One witness to an early nineteenth-century enquiry dismissively referred to St Saviour's as 'a very large and old building erected before the Reformation and used for Roman Catholic worship and procession ... incapable of adaptation to the worship of the present generation'. Engravings of the period show how inept the attempts to adapt it for Protestant parochial worship had been. It is unrecognizably crammed with screens, box pews and galleries. The stone altar screen in the sanctuary had been completely obscured by a baroque reredos and

The re-ordered choir of Southwark Cathedral showing Bishop Fox's sixteenth-century altar screen, which was restored in 1905 and decorated by Sir Ninian Comper in 1930. Comper also designed the stained glass.

the decaying nave had been cut off from the rest of the church by a solid wooden screen. In 1831 the parishioners decided that they could no longer afford the upkeep of this nave and unroofed it. They demolished what remained in 1839 and replaced it with a tawdry apology in the gimcrack Gothic style (Pugin lambasted it as 'as vile a preaching place as ever I did see'). A similar process of decay beset the handsome chapels to the east of the church. The so-called Bishop's Chapel had been leased to a baker in the time of Elizabeth I and was only restored to religious use by Bishop Andrewes in the 1620s. The chapel of St Mary Magdalene to the north was demolished in 1822 and the Bishop's Chapel was pulled down in 1830 in order to improve access to the new London Bridge. After this low point, the process of restoration was gradual, but generally sensitive. It was only in 1890–97 that the nave was rebuilt in a style deemed appropriate (its architecture derives from that of the surviving choir rather from what engravings show was there before 1839). The cathedral's fittings are particularly rich. Bishop Fox's great altar screen was particularly well restored in 1905 with statues of saints placed in its once empty niches (the lower part was

The alabaster Shakespeare Monument in the nave of Southwark Cathedral, constructed in 1911.

gilded in 1930 when Sir Ninian Comper added an altarpiece and bright blue and yellow stained-glass for the triple lancet windows above).

Elsewhere in the cathedral much is made of the local historical literary connections. The poet, John Gower, was buried here in 1408 and his over-restored, and over-painted, canopied tomb has somehow survived in the much-rebuilt nave. Opposite is a tomb-like monument to Shakespeare placed here in 1911. It shows the poet reclining, or rather dozing, against a background relief of the Bankside area in the 1600s. Shakespeare's younger brother, Edmond, was buried in St Saviour's in 1607, as were the play-wrights John Fletcher (1625) and Philip Massinger (1640), but none of the graves is now marked. A series of stained-glass windows on the north side of the new nave show Southwark's other literary connections (though, interestingly there is no reference to Charles Dickens). Perhaps the most extraordinary of Southwark Cathedral's recent fittings is the spectacular, gilded and multi-pinnacled Gothic tabernacle in what is now designated the 'Harvard Chapel'. What the soundly Protestant John Harvard might have thought of such

A ceiling boss from
Southwark Cathedral

Created by Icelandic artist, Leifur Breidfjord, this stained-glass window was installed on
the south side of the retro choir of Southwark Cathedral to commemorate the Diamond
Jubilee of Elizabeth II.

a patently Catholic intrusion can merely be speculated upon. The tabernacle is the work of Pugin and was shown by him in the Gothic Court of the Great Exhibition in 1851. It was installed in Pugin's own Catholic church of St Augustine at Ramsgate until it was unceremoniously disposed of during a re-ordering in 1971. It is now returned to its proper dignity and use, ironically, at the heart of an Anglican cathedral.

In 1931 Bishop Cyril Garbett of Southwark somewhat disparagingly described his cathedral as 'hidden away low down amidst the homes of poverty and the warehouses of modern commerce'. The cathedral on the banks of the Thames is still hemmed in, but now it is overshadowed by The Shard and the former 'homes of poverty', and the warehouses have largely been replaced by the tower of Guy's Hospital, by offices, hotels and apartments. Southwark had been designated a proto-cathedral of the Rochester Diocese in 1897 and elevated to full cathedral rank in 1905. Unlike the majority of other 'new' Anglican cathedrals it looks the part. After Southwark no other large medieval churches were either available or conveniently sited to serve as cathedrals. Nevertheless, since 1914 no fewer than ten new Anglican dioceses have been created and ten existing parish churches raised, sometimes only temporarily, to the rank of cathedral. With only three exceptions, these new cathedrals still occupy the pre-existing churches, albeit churches that have been enlarged or somehow 'enhanced'. Coventry's cathedral was destroyed in the Second World War and a daringly new church was built to replace it on an adjacent site, The diocese of Guildford resolved to build a new, large cathedral on a virgin site, and St Edmundsbury has so amply and extravagantly expanded its old church as to render it virtually a brand-new structure.

NEW CATHOLIC DIOCESES AND A CATHOLIC RE-ORDERING

The Roman Catholic Church in England has also created five new dioceses since 1917, but two of the new sees were able to inherit nineteenth-century churches of truly cathedralesque pretensions and proportions. Nevertheless, the history of Catholic cathedrals in the twentieth century has often been fraught. The challenge that beset many Catholic bishops in the mid-twentieth century was how to make their cathedrals conform to the liturgical and theological changes brought about by the Second Vatican Council which sat between 1962 and 1965. Those English bishops who attended the Council took their time to respond to these innovations, but their immediate successors certainly did not. In the case of most of the Catholic cathedrals all caution, and most aesthetic considerations, were thrown to the winds. Re-ordering became the order of the day. Although the authorities at many Anglican cathedrals responded to a similar pressure for architectural changes that reflected liturgical ones, they tended to be both more conservative and more sensitive to the quality of the historic churches in their charge. Anglican bishops have traditionally had little direct influence over their cathedrals. That responsibility fell to a dean and his chapter. Roman Catholic cathedrals, by contrast, have until recently had 'administrators' rather than 'deans' and it was the local bishop who possessed the real sway. Catholic cathedrals are essentially 'bishops' churches' and not the preserve of the administrative clergy.

Central to the 'modernization' of the liturgy was an emphasis on the Eucharist and on the visibility and audibility of the priest at the altar. Instead of facing east, with his back to the faithful, priests were now required to face their congregations. This generally meant either moving an exisiting altar forward or supplementing it with a second, free-standing altar. Many Catholic cathedrals also decided to return to the early-Christian practice of placing a bishop's *cathedra* prominently behind the altar rather than to one side of it. Some of these radical redefinitions of church interiors had taken place before the Second Vatican Council met, but to bishops returning from Rome, the progressive way forward was informed as much by ancient tradition as by modern theology. Some churchmen were wedded to all things modern, while others looked for a return to the early Roman model of how a bishop's church should be physically arranged. Although the great basilicas of Rome, except St Paul's, had either completely lost their early-Christian character or had had it coated in a Baroque veneer, all retained a prominent, highly visible, free-standing altar over a *confessio* (either a saint's tomb or a relic chapel). In Rome the presiding bishop (the Pope) tends to have his episcopal throne in the apse behind, an arrangement adopted from the precedent of an ancient Roman law-court. Such an arrangement is very different from that of the Gothic cathedrals of northern Europe. Although Romanesque and Gothic churches had initially developed from the basilican model, they tended to move to a cruciform shape with pronounced transepts. More significantly, the nave and the choir were divided from one another by a solid screen and with an altar at the east end standing against a wall or backed by an elaborate reredos. Mass was celebrated not only with the priest's back to his congregation, but with that congregation kept well away both from him and from the altar itself. In the 1960s and 1970s most English Catholic bishops found themselves with nineteenth-century churches built strictly according to medieval English or French models. Re-ordering them was therefore no easy matter. Hence the unfortunate, and often destructive, changes they insisted on making. A proper appreciation of Victorian architecture may then have been in its infancy, but this lack of architectural sympathy does not excuse the philistinism of many of the alterations. Given its non-Gothic style, and a good deal of tact, only Westminster Cathedral escaped a radical reorganization of its historic interiors. The twelve-ton granite altar, centred under Bentley's baldacchino, was so heavy that it seemed to be unmovable (the feat of providing sufficient space behind it for the celebrants was only achieved in time for the visit of Pope Benedict XVI in 2010). At Westminster too, the archbishop's throne remained where it had historically been, on the north side of the sanctuary. The Archbishop of Liverpool, too, already had a purpose-built cathedral equipped to embrace the liturgical changes. Other Catholic bishops may have yearned for a similarly unequivocally modern cathedral, but a combination of aesthetic insensitivity and a lack of adequate financial resources limited the scope and nature of their decisions.

MIDDLESBROUGH

When, in 1878, the original Catholic diocese of Beverley in Yorkshire was divided into the two new sees of Leeds and Middlesbrough the two bishops, and their successors, made very different decisions about their cathedrals. The first Bishop of Middlesbrough built himself an ample, if unlovely red-brick Gothic cathedral in Sussex Street in 1876–8. It lasted barely a hundred years. As the centre of Middlesbrough declined in the 1960s, and liturgical changes took hold, so the Gothic cathedral was allowed to decay. A decision to move to a new site was first mooted in 1976, and in 1985 a foundation stone was laid at Coulby Newham, some five miles to the south of the town. The unloved old cathedral has now been demolished after a distressing period of neglect and gradual ruination. Its successor, designed by Frank Swainston and Peter Fenton, is unapologetically modern in style and constructed according to the demands of post-Vatican Council recommendations, but it cannot be called inspiring.

LEEDS CATHEDRAL

The first bishops of Leeds were faced with quite different dilemmas. St Anne's Church, which was designated as the first cathedral, stood in Cookridge Street and had been built in 1838. This church was compulsorily purchased in 1899 by the City's Corporation and demolished in order to make way for a road-widening scheme connected with a new tramway system. The city gave the diocese a somewhat awkward, site 150 feet away along Cookridge Street.

The new cathedral, designed by J.H. Eastwood and Sydney Greenslade, was started in 1901 and was opened for its first Mass in May 1904 (before structural work had been fully completed). It was not consecrated until 1924 and has been re-ordered twice since (in 1924 and more disruptively in 1960–4). Its stonework was cleaned in 1987. Leeds Cathedral is basically a barrel-roofed square, but its architects were adept at dividing that square into distinct areas and giving an impression of uncluttered spaciousness. It is in a pleasingly free Arts-and-Crafts Gothic style and the detailing (mostly by Greenslade) is of an admirable quality. Its fittings are particularly handsome. The cathedral's interior is dominated by the high red and gold reredos of 1901. Just as beautiful is the painted and gilded altar-piece from the old cathedral designed by Pugin in 1842 and preserved in the Lady Chapel. It has large statues of St Anne and St Wilfred flanking the Virgin and Child and six angelic figures. The cultivated stiffness in these noble statues embodies everything that Pugin most admired about English Gothic sculpture, though, as he well knew, so very little of the medieval originals had survived the ravages of the Reformation.

LANCASTER CATHEDRAL

A Catholic diocese was created at Lancaster in 1924 and the new bishop selected the substantial, but suburban, church of St Peter as his cathedral. This church, with its elegant spire, was designed between 1857 and 1859 by the celebrated northern architect, Edward Paley. Alas, its interiors were wrecked by a mid-century re-ordering, but the effects of this drastic re-ordering were partially undone in 1995. The cathedral's finest, and most prominent, fitting is the lovely triptych-like panelled reredos, designed in 1909. It is an early work by Giles Scott, the architect of Liverpool's Anglican cathedral. It stands in what used to be the sanctuary, a space now divided from the nave by a metalwork screen, and designated as the Blessed Sacrament Chapel. The new, bland free-standing main altar and the nondescript bishop's throne thus are fortunate to have such a glorious backdrop.

CLIFTON CATHEDRAL, BRISTOL

One long-established Catholic diocese, Clifton, finally got the cathedral it had long hoped for only in 1973. The Bishop of Clifton's pro-cathedral, dedicated to the Holy Apostles, had been begun in the style of a lush Roman temple in 1834. It was to stand in the handsome, predominantly Classical, Bristol suburb of Clifton and would have been a noble complement to its surroundings. Unfortunately, when the money ran short in the 1840s the fragment of the Roman portico that had been built was unhappily transformed into a Romanesque façade. The distinctly unlovely church behind was only finished in 1876. Money remained a problem and even a drastic re-ordering that was contemplated in the 1960s had to be abandoned. Instead the old site was abandoned and a striking concrete church was constructed on a small four-acre plot in Pembroke Road. This new cathedral was a direct response to the radical liturgical changes introduced by the Second Vatican Council. Despite the heavy, pierced concrete beams that support its roof, the new cathedral is an airy series of uninterrupted spaces. The altar, which stands freely against a blank east wall, is dramatically lit by a high lantern. Externally, this lantern rises supported by concrete fins like some kind of sculptural sky-rocket. It is an infinitely more satisfying building than the new cathedral at Middlesbrough (which it superficially resembles).

BRENTWOOD CATHEDRAL

In 1991, less than twenty years after the dedication of Clifton, a far newer see built itself an utterly, and unexpectedly, different cathedral. The plan of the new cathedral at Brentwood in Essex (founded in 1917) reveals a similarly direct response to the demands of the new Catholic liturgy, but the radical architectural solution provided by its architect, Quinlan Terry, could not be more different. Bishop Thomas McMahon, who selected Terry as his architect, had a taste for the principles of Classical architecture and a clear vision of a dignified, historically referential, setting for the Mass. What Bishop McMahon wanted, and what he got, are described in the guidebook to the cathedral written by the bishop himself. The small Victorian Gothic church of St Helen of 1861, which had heretofore served as the cathedral, was retained but in place of its northern aisle Terry constructed a square Italianate hall lit by high round-headed windows and by an octagonal lantern. This 'hall' has a noble arcade of arches

188

supported by severe Tuscan columns and the supplementary aisles to the east and west have large Venetian windows in the eighteenth-century manner. The effect recalls a parish church by Wren or Gibbs (the long-lost St Bartholomew's-by-the-Exchange comes to mind) but without a pronounced apse or any gallery. Brentwood's interior planning is that of a modern Catholic church with a severe marble central altar barely raised above the level of the congregation by a single step. A Renaissance-style episcopal throne stands behind it, and an *ambo*, or reading desk, faces it. Apart from structural ornament, all other decorative detail has been kept to a minimum, giving the cathedral an almost Calvinist severity (something that doubtless appealed to the devoutly Protestant architect who believed that the Classical orders are divinely inspired). The surviving nave of the old church now serves as a Chapel of the Blessed Sacrament but even here objects of popular devotion, so common in Catholic churches, seem to have been rigorously excluded. In the main body of the cathedral the distinctly modern-style terracotta Stations of the Cross, by Raphael Maklouf, are subtly placed in roundels in the arcade. Outside, the Kentish ragstone of the walls, which continue the stonework of the Gothic church, is relieved with white Portland pilasters and a circular columned porch.

Our Lady and St Philip Howard, Arundel

In his guidebook to his new cathedral Bishop McMahon refers elusively to the 'Divine Providence' that provided the 'substantial sums of money ... that made a new cathedral possible'. His providentially generous donors remain anonymous.

Not so the prodigiously generous builder of the Catholic Church's two grandest new cathedrals, Arundel and Norwich. Both date from the late nineteenth century and both were paid for by Henry, the fifteenth Duke of Norfolk. These abnormally grand Gothic former parish churches became, respectively, the cathedrals of the dioceses of Arundel and Brighton (formed out of the Southwark see in 1967) and East Anglia (formed out of the Northampton see in 1976). Henry, Duke of Norfolk, whose premier

Thanks to the munificence of the Duke of Norfolk, the Catholic Cathedral of Our Lady and St Philip Howard at Arundel was grandly constructed in the years 1870–3. It was raised to cathedral rank in 1967.

seat is at Arundel Castle, was a devout Catholic, well aware of his family's historic loyalty to the Church and of the persecution to which members of his family had been subjected. In the north transept of the cathedral at Arundel is a shrine to St Philip Howard, the Earl of Arundel who had died, perhaps poisoned, in the Tower of London in 1595. The relics of St Philip, who was canonized in 1970, had formerly been enshrined in the Fitzalan Chapel, the private, Catholic, mausoleum of the family of the dukes attached to the nearby Anglican parish church of Arundel. They were brought to what had become a new cathedral in 1971, and two years later the dedication of the great church was changed to 'Our Lady and St Philip Howard'. Arundel Cathedral had been built in the French thirteenth-century style to the designs of J.A. Hansom between 1870–3. Hansom, who designed the lovely spires of the cathedrals of Plymouth and Newcastle, is perhaps best remembered as the originator of the 'Hansom Cab'. He was, however, a singularly gifted architect who was blessed with a deep Romantic strain. Seen from the meadows to its south, his cathedral and Arundel Castle, rise like some renewed vision of the lost feudal glories of the Middle Ages. The church was intended to mark the twenty-first birthday of Henry, fifteenth Duke of Norfolk, and was to be dedicated to another St Philip, the founder of the Oratorian Order, Filippo Neri (the duke had been educated by the Oratorians). Despite the fact that nineteenth-century English Oratorians had a distinct taste for Italianate rather than Gothic architecture, the duke demanded a church that would express both antiquity of his house and the unbroken witness of the Catholic Church in England.

Although the cathedral lacks the proposed north-west tower and an eastern Lady Chapel, it is still a magnificent sight from a distance. Sadly, the lack of the Lady Chapel renders the eastern end of the cathedral's interiors disappointingly anti-climactic (a fact that is not helped by its rather awkward re-ordering). Nevertheless, Arundel is undoubtedly one of the finest Catholic churches of its age and it now serves as one its most impressive modern cathedrals.

St John the Baptist, Norwich

The fifteenth Duke of Norfolk's cathedral at Arundel dominates the small town that also contains his castle. His church at Norwich is prominently sited in the much larger county town of the shire from which he derived his title. Again, the duke was munificent. He built a 275-foot long and 80-foot high church that was always set to rival the low-lying nearby Anglican cathedral, but though its delicately detailed bulk is of cathedralesque proportions, it was built merely as the substantial parish church of St John the Baptist. If it had only had a spire to crown its lowering tower, it would be easily mistaken for the ancient cathedral by an undiscriminating visitor.

Its bishop, as of 1976, has the title 'Bishop of East Anglia' rather than 'Bishop of Norwich'. The cathedral was begun in 1884 to the designs of the prodigiously talented George Gilbert Scott junior, the Catholic convert son of Sir Gilbert Scott (and, incidentally, the father of the future architect of Liverpool's Anglican cathedral). The younger Scott was only able to oversee the construction of the church's sturdy nave, in a strict early English style, before

The sanctuary in the Cathedral of St John the Baptist, Norwich.

succumbing to alcohol and illness (he resigned as architect in 1894, and died prematurely in 1897). The church was completed by his brother, John Oldrid Scott, and was finally consecrated in 1910. Impressive though its exterior is, the real splendour of the Cathedral of St John the Baptist lies in its finely proportioned, stone-vaulted interior. Some of the Victorian glass in its lancet windows was lost in the Second World War but what survives is of high quality and has an excellent, if subdued, colour. Another member of the Scott dynasty, Adrian Gilbert, designed the old high altar, but this was moved from the sanctuary as part of an inevitable mid-twentieth-century re-ordering.

SHEFFIELD HALLAM

The most recent Catholic diocese created in England is that of Sheffield Hallam. This new see, established in 1980, has as its cathedral the Church of St Marie, built by Matthew Hadfield between 1847 and 1850. It is a small building distinguished only by its Pugin glass in the east window and by its reredos of 1850 by the same architect.

ANGLICAN CATHEDRALS SINCE 1914

Sheffield's Anglican cathedral is the old parish church of the town, a relatively undistinguished building, partly rebuilt in the opening years of the nineteenth century and then confusingly tampered with over the course of the next one hundred and sixty years. It was thoroughly restored in the 1880s when the nave was lengthened and the transepts reconstructed, and then given a far more extensive 'makeover' after it was raised to cathedral rank in 1914. The work was done by Sir Charles Nicholson in the late 1930s, but was far from complete when Nicholson died in 1949. A new architectural programme was adopted in the 1960s, the chief merit of which is a lantern at the west end, the design of which suggests that its architects found difficulty in distinguishing between the medieval and the modern. The cathedral's interiors testify loudly to a confused pattern of construction and reconstruction and speak of awkward compromises rather than architectural single-mindedness.

The Church of England's ten new twentieth-century dioceses were spread across the country with an evident emphasis on serving the growing populations of the Midlands and the South. Three northern sees were created at Sheffield (1914), Bradford (1919) and Blackburn (1926). These were complemented by three Midlands dioceses: Coventry (a see resurrected after many centuries in 1918); Derby (established in 1927 in territory formerly part of the sees of Lichfield and Southwell); and Leicester (also 1927, taking Leicestershire out of the see of Lincoln). The Anglican Church also created four southern bishoprics starting with Chelmsford in Essex (carved out of the diocese of St Albans in 1913), St Edmundsbury and Ipswich in Suffolk (taken out of the sees of Ely and Norwich in 1914) and followed in 1927 by Portsmouth in Hampshire and Guildford in Surrey (both divisions of the extensive diocese of Winchester). Of these sees that of Bradford lost its distinct identity in 2013 when it was incorporated into the new Anglican bishopric of Leeds. Its cathedral, with the eastern arm added in the 1950s by Edward Maufe, retains its title though it was never merited comparison with the far finer churches at Ripon and Wakefield, which have shared its effective loss of status.

BLACKBURN

The first bishop of the Lancashire diocese of Blackburn inherited the parish church of St Mary as his cathedral. It dated only from 1820 but it had had to be reconstructed in a spindly Decorated Gothic style after a fire in 1831. St Mary's has quite pretty tiercon vaults (in plaster) that now contain stencilling in the medieval manner. When it was raised to cathedral rank plans were drawn up by W. A. Forsythe to expand the church, retaining only the nave and its west tower. Work began on a new eastern arm in 1938 but the advent of the Second World War did not allow building work to proceed far. In 1961 Lawrence King took over Forsythe's brief and abandoned a proposed octagonal tower and lantern due to rising costs. What we have instead is a *corona* over the crossing topped externally with spiky pinnacles and a thin apology for a spire. Internally, this corona gives space but relatively little aesthetic pleasure.

CHELMSFORD

The parish church of Chelmsford, which became a cathedral in 1913, was a much more elegant piece of historic architecture. That said, it was, and is, essentially a substantial East Anglian church of the late Middle Ages. Its tower, distinguished by a pretty eighteenth-century lantern, its handsome porch, and its flint-rubble exterior are attractive enough, but the sheer blandness of its interior has been accentuated by the rebuilding of the nave in 1800–3, by a heavy-handed restoration in 1862 and a yet more thoroughgoing one at the hands of Sir Arthur Blomfield in 1873 (when the north transept was built). A scheme to enlarge the cathedral was discussed in the 1920s but all that changed was the addition of two bays to the chancel and the construction of a block of vestries. The cathedral was re-ordered in 1983–4 which resulted in the introduction of a free-standing slate altar and a new bishop's throne at the east end.

PORTSMOUTH

Though it too was formerly a large parish church, Portsmouth's Anglican cathedral has been much more successfully transformed into a building worthy of the name 'cathedral'. The transformative process was particularly long drawn-out, but the end result is a happy example of what the twentieth-century church architect, Sir Ninian Comper, described as 'unity by inclusion'. Each distinct stylistic element of the church has been allowed to work in harmony with another and none makes a dominant statement.

Portsmouth Cathedral, like the city in which it stands, is a fascinating mixture of styles, and both city and church have had to endure many vagaries of urban definition, bombardment and reconstruction. St Thomas's only became a parish church in 1320 when the city's naval importance was becoming paramount. It anciently served Portsmouth proper, for, given its complex geography, the port city and the great naval dockyard sprawled over several neighbouring urban parishes. Since the nineteenth century, and even more so since the Second World War, the centre of modern Portsmouth has shifted away from the old High Street where the cathedral stands. St Thomas's now seems happily cut off from the busier areas around the city's Guildhall.

The oldest part of the present church, which was founded as a chapel dedicated to St Thomas à Becket by the Augustinian canons of Southwick Priory, dates from the late twelfth century. What remains is both bold and elegant and was clearly meant to proclaim the powerful virtues of the cult of the recently martyred saint. Another political murder is commemorated in the south choir aisle. The wall monument to the Duke of Buckingham, who was assassinated in a house in Portsmouth High Street in 1628, was later moved out of the chancel. It is probably the work of Nicholas Stone and is full of Baroque flourish and overstatement (so much so that a Victorian guidebook dismisses it as 'hideous').

The cathedral's medieval nave and the west tower were severely damaged by bombardment during the Civil War (when it was being defended by Royalists). Charles II subsequently promised to contribute to the ruined church's restoration, but no work was begun until 1683 and it was only completed ten years later. A new nave was constructed in a restrained Classical style and the new tower, jauntily capped by an octagonal lantern, was added. The tower remains a landmark for ferry-passengers sailing in and out of the port, though it now has to compete with slab-like blocks of apartments in the near distance. Internally, the juxtaposition of the handsome twelfth-century work in the choir and the late seventeenth-century nave is surprisingly pleasing.

After cathedral status had been granted in 1927 the church was expanded to the west by Sir Charles Nicholson in a stripped, rather plodding, Romanesque style (1935–9). The cathedral escaped major damage in the Second World War (though the surrounding area did not) and the scheme initiated by Nicholson had to wait until 1991 to be completed. There were considerable changes to the original plan but Michael Drury's architectural solution is generally successful. The twin towers of the western façade give the cathedral the look of a twelfth-century Germanic abbey but their playful Tudoresque lead ogee caps are unmistakeable reminders of those of the White Tower in the Tower of London.

DERBY

The Midland dioceses of Derby and Leicester, both founded in 1927, inherited very different but substantial parish churches as new cathedrals. All Saints, Derby, has a particularly noble western tower which is still the most interesting architectural feature on the city's skyline. It was built in the early sixteenth century and culminates in frilly battlements and fine, tall pinnacles. The rest of the church was rebuilt in the early 1720s to the designs of James Gibbs. This rebuilding was on the initiative of its rector, Dr Michael Hutchinson, who became so vexed at the indecisive responses of Derby's Corporation to the submitted estimates that he began the demolition himself on a February morning in 1723.

What Hutchinson got was a Classical church of some real sophistication. It follows the pattern of Gibbs's St Martin-in-the-Fields in London with its vault carried on Tuscan columns raised on pedestals. The proportions of the medieval collegiate church that preceded the present one are lost, but Gibbs and his builders, the Smith brothers of Warwick, recognized that the height of the new church should not unbalance the supremacy of the surviving steeple. Elegant though it is, there is a certain broad squatness about Derby Cathedral, both inside and out.

Not everything was new about its interior. Alert to the local and national importance of the family of the Dukes of Devonshire, Dr Hutchinson set aside a Cavendish Chapel in the south chancel aisle with a family vault beneath it. Here, most prominently, is the sumptuous monument to Elizabeth, Countess of Shrewsbury (Bess of Hardwick) designed in 1607 by Robert Smythson.

The cathedral was partly refitted in the 1890s by the architect,

Temple Moore, but far more important changes were made in 1967–72 when a two-bay eastern extension was added by Sebastian Comper (the son of Sir Ninian). Comper's design echoes Gibbs's, but the baldacchino in the new chancel, the organ case in the gallery and the touches of colour and gilding in the interior are decided innovations. The loveliest feature of the interior is the splendid wrought-iron screen that stretches across the chancel. It is the work of the local master, Robert Bakewell, and dates from 1730. Bakewell also made the communion rails and the stands for the Corporation's mace and sword. All Saints remains the self-evidently proud civic

Derby Cathedral, showing the early sixteenth-century tower and the eastern extension built 1967–72.

church of a thriving provincial town but it has very satisfyingly adapted itself to its role as bishop's cathedral.

It is sometimes said that 'Bonnie Prince Charlie' (Prince Charles Edward Stuart) heard Mass at All Saints in December 1745 during his brief sojourn in Derby shortly before beginning his retreat to Scotland. Although this sounds like an early gesture of assertive, if

Robert Bakewell's wrought-iron choir screen in Derby Cathedral dates from 1730.

uninvited, ecumenism, the story is most likely to be a fiction. Apart from the fact that such a Mass would have been a provocation of Anglican sensibilities, the Catholic chaplains of the Prince would probably have regarded the new All Saints as improperly consecrated.

Created by Ceri Richards in 1964 and installed in the north aisle of Derby Cathedral, this stained-glass window represents 'All Souls' and is one of a pair by the same designer, whose 'All Saints' can be viewed on the south aisle.

LEICESTER

A very difference spirit of ecumenism has played its part in establishing Leicester Cathedral's most significant royal connection. Uniquely amongst the younger generation of English cathedrals, Leicester contains the tomb of an English king. Richard III was killed at the Battle of Bosworth Field, near Leicester, in 1485. His mutilated body was brought into the city and given burial by its

Franciscan Friars in their now vanished church. This was evidently a boldly generous move, for Richard was damned as a tyrant, a murderer and a usurper by those who had defeated him in battle. The Tudor dynasty continued to disparage this last Plantagenet king (as we know from Shakespeare's play) and when the Franciscan church was demolished at the time of the Dissolution in the 1530s, the site of the interment of England's last medieval king was forgotten. The body was only discovered again after a forensic research of the long-lost foundations of the friary in 2013. As the University of Leicester had been involved in the process of discovery it was finally agreed to re-inter the King in Leicester's cathedral (though some latter-day apologists for Richard had considered York Minster a church more worthy of royal dignity). Richard's first interment was hugger-mugger, but it was probably accompanied by due Catholic ritual. His second funeral, in an Anglican church, was less exclusively Catholic, but almost certainly more dignified. The new tomb (2015) replaced an earlier memorial slab in the chancel beautifully lettered by David Kindersley in 1980.

St Martin's Cathedral in Leicester has other rich historic connections, and contains some ancient elements, but it is largely a successful Victorian re-creation. Its present tower and the tall spire over the crossing are the work of the architect Raphael Brandon and date from 1861–7 (though they replace the original Norman tower and the medieval spire). Brandon also rebuilt the chancel and its chapels, while the north and south aisles are the result of thorough 'restorations' by G.E. Street and J.L. Pearson, respectively. Most of the cathedral's internal fittings date from the period of the church's new status in 1927. These include a spiky bishop's throne, the choir stalls, and a pleasing wooden choir screen, all in a free late-Gothic style with gestures to Arts-and-Crafts detail. They were designed by Sir Charles Nicholson. The church was again re-ordered in 2015 when the old choir was screened off to provide a new chapel and a dedicated setting for Richard III's tomb.

In the 1920s and 1930s it was still considered proper that the newly designated cathedrals should be adapted and fitted according to the principles of the Victorian Gothic revival. A hundred years earlier A.W.N. Pugin had insisted that the 'Pointed' was the only

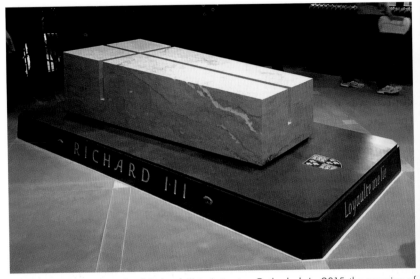

The newly designed tomb of Richard III in Leicester Cathedral. In 2015 the remains of the king were solemnly re-interred here in a ceremony that was televised and watched by a global audience.

Christian style and the architects that followed him firmly believed that the revival of the architecture of the Middle Ages was intrinsically linked to national identity. As we have seen, the Catholic cathedral at Westminster, built at the very end of the nineteenth century, broke church design out of the Gothic straitjacket, while Lutyens's proposed Metropolitan Cathedral at Liverpool would have emphatically reasserted the dynamism of the Classical. As the slow construction of the Liverpool Anglican cathedral showed, until the Second World War many twentieth-century church architects remained wedded to an increasingly free interpretation of medieval precedent. They also remained impervious to, and largely intolerant of, the revolution in church design taking place on the Continent. It was the Second World War, and the widespread destruction of British cities by bombing, which forcefully shifted established opinions as to how and why a church should be built and, moreover, what it should look like. The new cathedrals at Guildford and Coventry, contemporaries of one another, fall on different sides of this argument. The first boldly embodied a waning tradition. The second attempted to assert the importance of new stylistic and theological beginnings.

THE LATEST ANGLICAN CATHEDRALS

GUILDFORD

A new diocese of Guildford in Surrey was established in 1927, at the same time as those of Portsmouth, Derby and Leicester. Unlike those other cities, the new diocese considered its pro-cathedral, the eighteenth-century parish church of the Holy Trinity, both inadequate and architecturally undignified. The fact that Holy Trinity could not be easily enlarged was matched by a distaste for what was deemed to be its pedestrian architecture. A virgin site was acquired on Stag Hill to the north-west of the town and an open architectural competition for a design for a new cathedral was held in 1932. Out of 183 entries the winner was Edward Maufe (originally Muff), known primarily as the designer of two successful suburban churches and of villas in the sub-Modern style. Maufe's subdued, stripped brick Gothic

Guildford Cathedral from the west showing the porches completed 1965–6, the last part of the cathedral to be finished.

The nave of Guildford Cathedral looking towards the high altar.

design was decidedly conservative, but it is doubtful that any church on such a scale could have had a bolder design anywhere else in Europe (with the possible exception of Scandinavia).

Work began on the east end of the new cathedral in 1936 but building operations were suspended during the Second World War and only commenced again in 1952. Thus, though its design is emphatically *pre*-war, Guildford Cathedral is generally considered to be a church of the 1960s and will always be (adversely) judged as such.

The chancel and crossing were opened in 1954; the nave followed in 1961; and the cathedral was consecrated in May 1961. The western arcades and porches were completed only in 1964.

Guildford Cathedral has a dramatic enough profile when seen from a distance or from the railway. Its crossing tower, which one critic describes as 'unfinished-looking', has none of Liverpool's shapely splendour, but the golden angel on a spike at its crest is striking (especially so when it is floodlit after dark). The first impression made by the plain vaulted interior of the cathedral is one of placid and uniform dignity. Alas, that first impression remains the only lasting impression. Guildford Cathedral immediately proclaims what its architecture is about and then says nothing more. The cathedral's fittings do not help to lift the spirit, and the 17-m curtain behind the high altar is of the blandest beige (though some prefer to describe it as 'golden'). Its very neutrality somehow sums up the whole church building.

COVENTRY

The new cathedral at Guildford was what many liberal-minded, but otherwise traditional, Anglicans of the 1930s considered to be the ideal of English church architecture. It had the shape and substance of an historic cathedral, while cautiously proclaiming a spiritual-ity that was unencumbered by too much flummery. It was, as the Church of England liked to say of itself, 'Catholic and Reformed'. Thirty years later its critics readily complained that its time had passed. The new Coventry Cathedral was, however, what a new generation of liberal-minded, untraditional Anglicans demanded as a cathedral for the post-war age. It, too, is now a period piece. In the early 1960s it was hailed as daringly innovative, but it, and its wonderful fittings, now look inflexibly trapped in the decade that once rejoiced in its own 'modernity'.

The diocese of Coventry was revived in 1918. It had been an independent see from 1102 until it was joined to that of Lichfield in 1239. (Even then, the Bishops of Lichfield abandoned the title 'Lichfield and Coventry' only in 1836.) The Norman cathedral at Coventry, a monastic foundation, was completely destroyed at the time of the Dissolution, though fragments of the foundations of its east end were uncovered in 1955. When the first new Bishop of Coventry was appointed in October 1918 he chose as his cathedral the magnificent medieval parish church of St Michael.

St Michael's, with the churches of Holy Trinity and St John the Baptist, stand as testimony to prosperity of the city in the fourteenth and fifteenth centuries. The spires of St Michael's and Holy Trinity

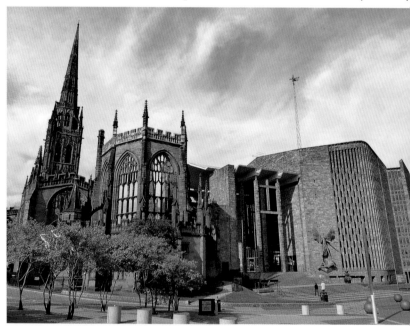

The new Coventry Cathedral juxtaposed with the ruins of the old. The cathedral is dedicated to the Archangel St Michael, who is represented in Jacob Epstein's striking statue by the entrance.

still dignify the city's otherwise commonplace modern skyline and some mean-minded commentators have always wondered why Holy Trinity was not allowed to assume cathedral status in the 1940s, following the destruction of its rival. Apart from its spire, the Cathedral of St Michael's was burned out and left a sad ruin in November 1940. This ruination, the result of the highly destructive and extended *blitzkrieg* on Coventry, gave the cathedral something of the aura of martyrdom. It first became a symbol of the inhumanity of war and then proclaimed itself part of a post-war process of reconciliation. By 1950 the re-creation of St Michael's became a moral necessity rather than a luxury.

The first plans for rebuilding the cathedral were sketched by Giles Scott (who was still involved with his work at Liverpool). When Scott withdrew in 1947 it was decided to hold a competition to find an architect who would be responsible for the design of an entirely new church, rather than for the partial restoration of the old one. The winning architect, Basil Spence, used the scarred walls and spire of the ruined church as a kind of forecourt to his new building. Thus the dead church has been allowed to stand as a prelude to the living church. Work was begun in 1954, though a foundation stone was not to be laid (by Elizabeth II) until 1956. The new cathedral was consecrated, in the presence of the Queen, on 25 May 1960, though work on the building was not fully completed for a further two years. The consecration was heralded as an event of international significance. Five days after the ceremony the cathedral hosted the first performance of Benjamin Britten's *War Requiem*, an impassioned comment on 'the pity of war' and a complex union of English poetry, Latin liturgy and music. It had been commissioned four years earlier in anticipation of the celebrations. To stress the cathedral's key role in the process of post-war reconciliation it had been hoped that the soloists in the *Requiem* would themselves be international (a Briton, a German and a Russian). It was not to be. At the last moment the Soviet Government refused permission for the Russian soloist to sing and her place had to be taken by another Briton. This was gesture politics in the most negative sense.

From the inception of the building project at Coventry it was intended that the new cathedral should display the very best in the arts that modern Britain could produce. Architecture, the graphic arts, sculpture and music would be united in showing a way forward, an aesthetic way as much as a theological one. The most immediate indicator of this 'new direction' is the orientation of Spence's cathedral. The ruins face towards the east; but the new, differently orientated structure abuts it on the north side of the old chancel. A flight of steps leads up the entrance porch, to the right of which is the striking bronze sculpture of a wide-eyed St Michael hovering triumphantly over a recumbent Lucifer. It is a late work by Jacob Epstein. The 'west' wall of the cathedral is a 70-foot high screen of glass in which the ruins are reflected. This screen is a re-interpretation of the tall Perpendicular windows of the old church, but here the openings are of bronze rather than stone tracery and they are filled with engraved rather than stained glass. The strikingly beautiful etched figures of angular saints and gyrating angels are the work of John Hutton.

The interior of the cathedral is completely dominated by the huge tapestry of Christ in Glory designed by Graham Sutherland. It is probably the finest, and certainly the largest, Modern work of art in any English cathedral. The effect is breathtaking. Sutherland's palette of colours is vibrantly exciting, the predominantly green background framing an almond-shaped *mandorla* in which a giant white-clad Christ sits in a pose of blessing, displaying His wounded hands and feet. Around the glorified Christ are the tangled, almost abstract representations of the four Beasts of the Apocalypse. Directly above the altar is a crucifixion scene and above that a chalice both stressing the nature of the eucharistic sacrifice offered below. The sheer scale of the figure of the Saviour is brought home by the life-sized figure of a naked human between His feet. The steady gaze of this *Pantocrator* recalls that of the mosaic Christ figures in the apses of the Byzantine and Norman churches of the Mediterranean.

It is only from the altar end that the architecture of the cathedral fully reveals itself. The windows of the single cell nave are set at an angle so that their light is directed towards this (ritual) east end. The shifting colours of the stained glass from window to window also forms a steady movement towards the altar, from restlessness to divine enlightenment. From this angle both the success and the

The nave of Spence's new Coventry Cathedral showing the stained glass and the great tapestry of Christ in Glory, designed by Graham Sutherland.

limitations of Spence's design become fully evident. The thin piers that divide the minimal aisles from the body of the nave rise up to support what is unmistakeably a version of a lierne vault. Here, as elsewhere, we can sense the ghost of a medieval structure that haunts the Modernist one. There is no faulting the elegance and the engineering, and there is no doubting that this is a building of the second half of the twentieth century, but Coventry is essentially a re-interpretation of the past rather than a radical departure from it.

St Edmundsbury Cathedral

The last English cathedral to be completed is unashamedly and unequivocally in the Gothic style. The diocese of St Edmundsbury and Ipswich was established just as the First World War began in August 1914. Ipswich was by far the bigger town but the choice of

St Edmundsbury Cathedral from the east, showing the central tower, which was completed in 2005.

Bury St Edmunds, with a population of 16,785, as the cathedral city was dictated by tradition. Tradition has continued to dictate virtually everything about the cathedral since it was so designated. Bury St Edmunds (as the town, if not the diocese, styles itself) was the creation of one of the great Benedictine abbeys of Europe. At the peak of its prosperity it was the fifth largest monastery in the Christian world and its abbey church was rivalled only in size by the cathedrals of Winchester and Old St Pauls. Of that great abbey, with its far-famed relics of St Edmund, only desultory fragments of flint wall survive. One notable grave, that of Henry VIII's sister, Mary, was moved from the abbey to St Mary's parish church, but there is little else to remind us of the great abbey's lost prestige. The town that grew up outside the abbey's walls boasted two handsome parish churches and the great Perpendicular naves of both are superb examples of the suave architectural confidence of East Anglia in the late Middle Ages. St Mary's Church also has a chancel worthy of its ten-bay nave. Not so St James's, which became the cathedral in 1914. Its superbly austere nave was begun c.1510 by the architect, John Wastell, the designer of the vaults of King's College Chapel at Cambridge and of the wonderful Bell Harry tower of Canterbury Cathedral. The nave was not finished until the 1550s after Edward VI gave £200 towards its completion (royal patronage had perforce replaced that of the redundant abbot, who had been generously pensioned off twenty years earlier with £330).

The medieval church of St. James was considerably altered in 1862–4 when Sir Gilbert Scott completely rebuilt the chancel and added the present open hammer-beam roof in the nave, thereby radically altering its pitch. Scott's alterations meant changes to Wastell's west façade (which directly fronts the street) and to the fenestration in the north and south aisles. Thus, when discussions about giving St James's more of the air of a cathedral were first held, the authorities were well aware that only one element of their church was ancient and therefore semi-sacrosanct. All plans for expansion were also restricted by the fact that the even more sacrosanct, if desultory, remains of the abbey's great façade stood directly to the east of St James's chancel.

In 1945 the 42-year-old Stephen Dykes Bower was appointed

as the architect for an expansion of the Cathedral. Dykes Bower was one of the last children of the Gothic Revival, a man devoutly respectful both of medieval precedent and of his Victorian predecessors. Although he proposed demolishing Scott's chancel, he suggested saving elements of it for later reuse. He was especially anxious to preserve and re-set the best of the old chancel's stained glass – two windows by C.E. Kempe of 1867 and 1874.

The plans for the first scheme of enlargement were published in 1953, according to which a new five-bay choir would be constructed to the east in place of Scott's work and a number of ancillary rooms added to the north of the church. This design envisaged a low tower, crowned by a copper pyramid and spirelet, over a newly created crossing. The fact that this design was unequivocally in the Gothic style caused uproar in the architectural press. The prejudices of the architectural establishment in this period were insistently, and moralistically, Modernist and the use of any historically referential style was commonly regarded as both benighted and as an insult to

St Edmundsbury Cathedral from the south, showing the twentieth-century crossing tower, the sixteenth-century nave and the surviving Romanesque abbey gateway.

212

the zeitgeist. With hindsight, the criticism of Dykes Bower's scheme for St Edmundsbury's Cathedral seems misguided. Sixty years on, very few critics would be prepared to admire an assertively Brutalist or astylar piece of architecture joined in a forced marriage to William Wastell's elegant nave. Admittedly, Dykes Bower was working next to a ruin, but, unlike Spence at Coventry, the ruin was not actually that of the cathedral that he had been called upon to expand.

Work on St Edmundsbury Cathedral began in 1960 starting with a north-west porch that would provide access from the street to the church and to a new cloister. From this cloister a number of vestries and meeting rooms would in future lead. Seven years later the choir was complete and in 1970 it and the transepts were consecrated. Dykes Bower's flat, triple-arched east wall is pierced by a trio of windows filled with some of the reused Victorian stained glass. The high altar beneath is decked with the wonderful gilt cross designed in 1932 by W.D. Caröe and the two candlesticks made in 1955 to match it. In the apex of the central arch above the altar Dykes Bower inserted a delicate wrought iron 'reredos', crowned with a sunburst and inlaid with semi-precious stones. The main, free-standing altar, in accordance with modern liturgical practice, is placed in the middle of the crossing with the choir stalls to its east. Dykes Bower's church is unapologetically planned as a reduced version of a great medieval cathedral, with distinct nave and choir areas, but there is no screen. Instead, the unbroken movement from west to east seems to pause in this crossing lit both from above and by the high windows in the tower and the transepts.

Dykes Bower died in 1994 with his cathedral unfinished and the proposed central tower rising only to the ridge level of the roofs. Recognizing how important his work on the cathedral had been to him, the architect left the greater part of his estate to it in the hope that work might continue. With the crucial support of the Millennium Commission, and funds from the National Lottery, St Edmundsbury Cathedral was declared a 'Millennium Project', enabling work to resume on a central tower designed by Hugh Matthew. The tower was completed in July 2005 and in June 2009 the new cloisters and crypt were consecrated. At the beginning of his transformation of the cathedral Dykes Bower had sanctioned the bright re-colouring of Scott's angel roof in the nave. The effect parallels the architect's colour schemes at Westminster Abbey (where he was surveyor from 1951 until his death). He also coloured the roof of his new choir and the scheme has been continued into the, admittedly garish, decoration of the posthumously designed fan-vaulted ceiling of the new tower.

The new fan vault over the crossing in St Edmundsbury Cathedral, designed in the opening years of the twenty-first century after the death of the cathedral's architect, Stephen Dykes Bower.

The transformation of St James's parish church into a cathedral has not always been a steady or uninterrupted process. What has ultimately been achieved, however, is something of an *amende honorable* for the loss of the old abbey church. In earlier centuries the great monastery churches at Gloucester, Peterborough and St Albans had been given new vocations as cathedrals. There was no surviving abbey church at Bury St Edmund's. The new cathedral is relatively small compared to its ancient rivals but, with its delicately proportioned new tower piercing the skyline, the cathedral now asserts what seems to be a rightful and properly ordained presence in the surrounding townscape.

7

THE CATHEDRAL IN THE MODERN WORLD

ANACHRONISTIC AS IT MIGHT seem to some critics, the cathedral at Bury St Edmunds proclaims the vitality of Gothic architecture in an age that has all too often assumed that the Gothic style died with the Plantagenets. The new parts of this cathedral were constructed by methods familiar to the early Tudor masons who had built the nave, their methods kept alive in subsequent centuries by those whose duty it had been to keep ancient buildings in a good state of repair. But this newest of Gothic cathedrals is also very much a functional church of the twenty-first century. The cathedral church proper is a series of interconnected, handsome and flexible spaces designed for dignified modern worship and ceremonial, but its adjacent ancillary buildings provide the kind of facilities now regarded as essential by clergy, worshippers and visitors alike. There are vestries and meeting rooms, a song school, a library, a book/ souvenir shop and a 'refectory' catering for both parishioners and tourists. Crucially – and mundane as it may at first seem – there are accessible lavatories. The older cathedrals have had to find or make space for similar facilities, but those at Edmundsbury's are purpose-built and integral to the church. Durham and Westminster Abbey have their bookshops, exhibition spaces, and refectories in parts of the old monastery buildings. Salisbury squeezes its café into an exhilarating, partially concealed space between the cloister and the nave; York, its lavatories into a Gothic-style extension hidden behind its chapter house; while St Albans and Southwark have been obliged to build architecturally sympathetic extensions to house meeting rooms and refectories. That relative youngster, the hundred-year-old Westminster Cathedral, with its large attached Archbishop's House, Clergy House, Choir School and Parish Hall, only provided adequate lavatory facilities for its worshippers and visitors in 2012. A modern cathedral is now much more than the exclusive preserve of its bishop and the clergy of its close, and the multitude of visitors that the great churches now attract require infinitely more comfort, diversion and instruction than did a medieval pilgrim.

It should never be forgotten that the English cathedrals of the twenty-first century remain primarily the seat of a diocesan bishop and the centre of his activities. Compared to their eighteenth- and nineteenth-century predecessors, latter-day bishops are very active in the life of their cathedrals. Absenteeism, in the manner of the grander Tudor, Caroline and Georgian prelates, became unacceptable in the nineteenth century, even when, for senior Anglican bishops, the business of the House of Lords might still claim precedence. It is now generally assumed that the diocesan will both celebrate and preach in the cathedral on the great Christian feasts of Christmas and Easter. Where a Victorian bishop was more likely to ordain clergy in his private chapel than in his cathedral, modern ordinations are very public ceremonies and are treated as great events in the life of a diocese and its people. Cathedrals are now regularly used for the consecration of new bishops, and in January 2015 the Church of England's first woman bishop was ordained by the Archbishop of York at York Minster in the presence of a large number of fellow bishops, priests and a substantial, sympathetic lay congregation.

On Maundy Thursday, the Thursday before Easter, all Catholic and many Anglican cathedrals assemble all of the diocesan clergy to witness the bishop's blessing of the holy oils used for anointing the newly baptized, the sick, the newly consecrated and the ordained. On a rotation principle, the distribution of the Royal Maundy Money takes place annually in one of the Anglican cathedrals on the Thursday before Easter. The ancient service has long lost the ceremonial foot-washing once performed by the reigning monarch, but the act of presenting alms to the elderly in the form of specially minted silver coins has survived. By the reign of Queen Victoria the ceremony was rarely attended by the monarch and was generally held either in one of the Chapels Royal or at Westminster Abbey with a royal almoner officiating in place of the monarch. The Royal Maundy Service was revived in its present form only in 1932 and since the beginning of the reign of Elizabeth II has generally taken place at one of the great churches outside London (including the cathedrals at St David's and Armagh). The Established Church of England remains faithful to its historic links to the Crown and the great cathedrals have become central to national commemorations. In London, of course, St Paul's Cathedral vies with Westminster Abbey as the accepted setting for royal weddings, state funerals, jubilees and national services of thanksgiving or public mourning. It was at St Paul's that Victoria celebrated her Golden and Diamond Jubilees and similar ceremonies have been observed to mark significant anniversaries in the reigns of George V and Elizabeth II. St Paul's also provided the magnificent setting for the state funerals of Nelson, Wellington and Churchill.

In recent decades all of the English cathedrals have developed as a vital element in Christian identity; a Christian identity that is often content to be recognized as 'national'. Cathedrals act as focal points, as much within a diocese as within the nation as a whole, but they provide more than a grand setting for state celebration or national mourning. Cathedral culture has moved on since the poet T.S. Eliot somewhat narrowly defined 'the value and use of cathedrals in England' in a lecture he gave at Chichester Cathedral in 1954:

A cathedral is a kind of monastic institution open to the public: and the attendance of the public is only important, if important at all, when there is some ceremony which concerns the whole diocese or the whole province or perhaps the whole nation.

Many Anglican cathedrals have now assumed the very public role of glorified and glorious parish churches, offering high standards of choral worship on weekdays and Sundays alike. It is not just

ourists and visitors who swell the number of Sunday worshippers
in English cathedrals. As T.S. Eliot also argued: 'it is the function
of the cathedral to maintain the highest standards of religious art
and music.' They have certainly fulfilled Eliot's hopes. New generations of worshippers have been drawn steadily to a spiritual ethos
of those cathedrals that are able to outclass that offered by local
churches which can command only limited resources in terms of
their clergy, choirs and fine architecture. Few of these new regular
worshippers in cathedrals appear to worry about a watered-down
sense of a parish community or of the neighbourly intimacy that
the old parish churches once exclusively claimed. The Catholic
cathedrals have earned a similar loyalty and have successfully cultivated their new role as flourishing parishes in their own right. The
Catholic churches continue the long tradition of opening for long
hours for daily, private prayer and for set times of public worship.
Even those historical Anglican cathedrals that charge an entry fee
for visitors preserve accessible areas, generally where the Sacrament
is reserved, where silent prayer is welcomed and free access is available. No cathedral has yet dared to charge for attendance at daily
offices or Sunday worship.

It will never be fully possible to distinguish between 'visitors' to
cathedrals and those who prefer to think of themselves as latter-
day 'pilgrims'. Certain historic centres of Christian pilgrimage
– Jerusalem, Rome or Santiago di Compostela – have an unbroken
tradition of coping with large numbers of devout visitors, some of
whom have taken ancient roads to their goals or have arrived on
foot for the last stage of an arduous and prayerful journey. Not
so those English cathedrals, notably Canterbury, which have lost
the relics that once fired prospective pilgrims with enthusiasm
and which inspired those who prayed at the tombs of the saints.
Geoffrey Chaucer's socially various group of pilgrims who set off
from Southwark seeking 'the holy blissful martyr' at Canterbury
would now be sadly disappointed with the brutally vacated spaces
in the cathedral.

Nevertheless, the tombs of St Cuthbert and St Bede at Durham,
devoid of their medieval splendour but not of their relics, still draw
the faithful to prayer, meditation and re-dedication. Other great

churches, notably Westminster Abbey and St Albans, make a point of marking the feast days of their respective saints with pilgrimage, prayer and due ceremony. Rainy days on the coast may well increase visitor numbers at Chichester, Truro or Exeter Cathedrals, but many of those who come to admire those great churches admit to being drawn into a sense of the numinous. These are pilgrims who may possess no defined religious goal but who nonetheless respond with a wonderment akin to a spiritual uplift.

Tourists and pilgrims alike now require the kind of comforts and facilities that are not narrowly associated with acts of worship. As we have seen, cathedrals are fully alert to the need to serve as flexible 'venues' for choral and orchestral concerts, for plays, recitals, lectures, debates and readings. Not all of these have a narrowly Christian, or even 'religious' orientation. As the largest roofed and heated space in many provincial cities this is not a new vocation for the local cathedral, but it is certainly a much appreciated one and one that adds vividly to the life and the broader mission of the churches concerned.

In this book I have looked exclusively at Anglican and Catholic cathedrals in England. As I noted in the Introduction they are no longer the *only* English cathedrals, though not one of them can be said to rival the size and architectural pretensions of the ancient cathedrals. The very word 'cathedral' still generally carries with it historic associations of splendour, serenity and grand proportions. Recently, certain dioceses have even taken to designating any large church a 'minster' whether or not it had ever held that historic dignity. A 'minster' was properly a former abbey or collegiate church (as with the cases of Ripon and Beverley). Not all of the ancient English cathedrals are as memorably distinctive as Durham or Ely, and even fewer have the architectural inventiveness of Lincoln or Wells or Gloucester or the sheer presence of St Paul's. Even amongst the nineteenth- and twentieth-century cathedrals only a handful could be said to approach the power of Westminster or Liverpool. Half a millennium ago great bishops remained powers in the land and their cathedral churches were required to reflect their greatness and the prestige of a mighty national Church. Very few modern bishops aspire to temporal power and very few modern states would

welcome their aspirations. In modern Britain, with its plural political and social make-up, no Church and no bishop would lay claim
to an unqualified or unquestioned influence in national affairs.
Many cathedrals now are of a size that would have been considered
more than adequate by the missionaries who first brought the faith
to England. Those early missionaries believed that cathedrals were
centres of prayer, meditation and teaching and, supremely, the living
focus of a bishop's pastoral activities. Essentially, therefore, nothing
has changed.

GLOSSARY

ABBEY a religious house belonging to a community such as the BENEDICTINES ruled over by an ABBOT.

ABBOT the superior of a religious house (*fem.* abbess).

AISLE the subsidiary space alongside the body of a church, separated from it by columns or piers.

APSE the semi-circular or polygonal space projecting at the end of church' nave generally containing the main altar.

ARCHBISHOP the metropolitan BISHOP who has jurisdiction over a PROVINCE of the Church. In England there are two provinces of the Anglican Church (Canterbury and York) and four in the Roman Catholic Church (Westminster, Southwark, Birmingham and Liverpool).

BALDACCHINO the free-standing canopy above an altar.

BASILICA originally a Roman public hall with aisles and an apse which contained the seat of a magistrate. The form of these halls was adapted for the earliest Christian churches in the Catholic tradition. The title 'basilica' is now given by the Pope to certain privileged churches such as St Peter's in Rome and St Mark's in Venice.

BAY the regular division of an interior space generally defined by an arch or window.

BENEDICTINES an order of monks following the Rule of St Benedict. Having been introduced to England by Augustine of Canterbury, the Rule of St Benedict was established in the north by St Wilfrid and was observed by most of the greater monasteries and in the monastic cathedrals (including Canterbury, Durham and Ely). Carlisle was served by Augustinian canons.

BISHOP the highest order of Christian minister ruling over a DIOCESE

BUTTRESS a vertical support projecting from a wall in order to stabilize it or to resist the vertical thrust of a vaulted roof. A flying buttress transmits this thrust by means of an arch or half-arch.

CAMPANILE a free-standing bell-tower.

CANON a member of the CHAPTER of a CATHEDRAL or COLLEGIATE CHURCH.

CANONIZATION the official declaration of sainthood by the Church. Following canonization the saint is allotted a Feast Day and can be venerated and invoked. Churches can also be dedicated to God in the name of a specific saint.

CATHEDRA a bishop's throne. The term derives from the Latin *cathedra* (a chair with arm-rests).

CATHEDRAL a bishop's church containing the bishop's CATHEDRA.

CHANCEL the east end of a church containing the main altar and formerly set aside for the use of the officiating clergy. It was often divided from the NAVE by a screen.

CHANTRY CHAPEL a chapel screened or partitioned off from the main body of a church endowed by its founder as a space where Mass could be said for the repose of his or her soul. Chantries were suppressed in English churches by an Act of 1547.

CHAPTER the assembly of the members of a religious house meeting in the CHAPTER HOUSE. In a SECULAR CATHEDRAL the CHAPTER members of the corporate body responsible for the spiritual and temporal concerns of the cathedral (the members are known as CANONS or PREBENDARIES and are supervised by the DEAN).

CHAPTER HOUSE the detached meeting room for the CHAPTER of a monastic church and for the canons of a secular cathedral. Chapter houses can be oblong in shape (as at Canterbury and Exeter) or polygonal (as at Wells and Salisbury). They are generally on the north side of the NAVE and situated off the CLOISTERS.

CHOIR the eastern part of a cathedral or monastery church containing the high altar and the seats of the clergy and the choir. As with a CHANCEL, the choir was often divided from the NAVE by a screen (hence CHOIR SCREEN).

CHOIR SCREEN the wooden, metal or stone screen dividing the CHOIR of a cathedral from the NAVE. A stone screen is sometimes referred to as a PULPITUM.

CHOIR STALLS the fixed seats of the clergy and the choir in the CHOIR of a cathedral. Usually these seats are joined together and have arm-rests and canopies.

CIBORIUM a fixed canopy over the altar; also known as a BALDACCHINO.

CLERESTORY the uppermost storey of the NAVE of a church pierced by windows.

CLOISTERS the enclosed, covered walkway forming the central part of a monastery. A cloister consists of a garth, or open plot or garden, surrounded on all four sides by broad, covered arcades. The term is derived from the Latin *claustrum* ('enclosed space'). Fine monastic examples survive at Canterbury, Durham and Gloucester Cathedrals, though cloisters are also a feature of some secular cathedrals (notably Salisbury).

COLLEGIATE CHURCH a church served by a 'college' of priests.

COMMUNION TABLE a wooden table, replacing or substituting for a stone altar, and used for the celebration of Holy Communion. A term preferred by sixteenth- and seventeenth-century Protestants.

CONFESSIO technically, the tomb of a martyr but more commonly used to describe the structure over such a tomb or of a CRYPT under the high altar containing relics.

CRYPT an underground area usually below the eastern part of a church.

CUPOLA a dome.

DEAN the head of a cathedral CHAPTER who ranks next to the BISHOP.

DECORATED the English Gothic style that flourished *c*.1290–1350. The term is derived from the type of window TRACERY used in the period.

DIOCESE the territorial unit of administration in the church ruled over by a bishop.

DORMITORY the former communal sleeping quarters of a monastery.

EARLY ENGLISH the English Gothic style prevalent *c*.1190–1250.

EPISCOPAL pertaining to a bishop (from the Latin *episcopus*, meaning 'bishop').

FAN VAULT a form of barrel vault evolved during the Perpendicular period, made up of fan-like masonry cones decorated with blind tracery.

FERETORY the part of the shrine of a saint containing the holy relics.

GALILEE CHAPEL a chapel usually at the west end of a CATHEDRAL (as at Durham).

GARGOYLE a sculpted waterspout carved to represent an animal or grotesque human figure.

HIERARCHY the ordered body of Christian ministers consisting of bishops, priests and deacons but often generally applied solely to the rule of diocesan bishops.

LADY CHAPEL the chapel dedicated to Our Lady (the Blessed Virgin Mary) most commonly situated to the east of the high altar in a cathedral, though in some cases it is partly detached from the body of the cathedral (as at Ely) or sited to the west (as in the Galilee at Durham).

LANCET WINDOW a slender, single-light, pointed-arched window which was a common feature of the EARLY ENGLISH style.

LANTERN the windowed stage of the crossing tower lighting the central space of a cathedral interior.

LIERNE VAULT liernes are short decorative ribs in the crown of a vault. Liernes are not linked to any springing point. A stellar or star-vault has liernes in a star formation.

METROPOLITAN an archbishop exercising authority over an ecclesiastical PROVINCE.

MISERICORD a shelf on a carved bracket on the underside of a hinged seat in the CHOIR STALLS, which supported the standing occupant of the stall during long services. The term is derived from the Latin *miserere* ('have mercy'). Misericords are often ingeniously carved, such as those at Norwich Cathedral.

MITRED ABBOT in medieval England an ABBOT who shared the status of a BISHOP and who sat as a peer in the House of Lords.

MULLION a vertical member dividing the lights of a Gothic window.

NARTHEX an enclosed vestibule or porch at the west end of a church.

NAVE the body of the church to the west of the crossing and the CHOIR, generally flanked by aisles. The term probably derives from the Latin *navis* ('ship').

NORMAN an alternative term for the ROMANESQUE style of architecture current in England under the Norman kings in the eleventh and twelfth centuries.

OGEE a double curve, bending first one way and then the other, forming an ogee arch.

ORATORY a private chapel in a church.

PERPENDICULAR the English Gothic style prevalent in the period *c*.1335–1530.

PEW seating for the laity outside the CHOIR (uncommon in English cathedrals).

PISCINA a stone basin, provided with a drain, for the cleansing of Mass vessels and generally set into a wall to the south of an altar.

PORTICO the columned porch to the west of a Classical church, the most spectacular example being the portico designed by Inigo Jones for old St Paul's.

PREBEND originally part of the revenue of a CATHEDRAL assigned to a particular CANON (who was known as a prebendary). The term prebend is now often interchangeable with that of CANON (though it survives in cathedrals such as Durham).

PRESBYTERY the part of a CATHEDRAL situated to the east of the CHOIR containing the high altar.

PRIOR the deputy head of a monastery. The position was of great significance in the abbey-cathedrals where the BISHOP held the title of ABBOT.

PROVINCE a group of dioceses forming an ecclesiastical unit under the jurisdiction of an ARCHBISHOP or METROPOLITAN.

PULPIT the raised stand, in wood or stone, for a preacher or reader. The term derives from the Latin *pulpitum* ('platform'), but it is not to be confused with PULPITUM (below).

PULPITUM a stone CHOIR SCREEN that separates the NAVE from the CHOIR.

REREDOS a painted or sculpted screen behind and above an altar.

RETABLE a painted or carved panel behind and above an altar and usually attached to it.

RETROCHOIR the area in a cathedral between the PRESBYTERY and an eastern LADY CHAPEL. In some instances (for example, Winchester and Saint Albans) it contained the shrine of a saint.

ROMANESQUE the eleventh- and twelfth-century architectural style often known in England as NORMAN.

ROOD a carved image of the crucified Christ with the Virgin Mary to His right and St John to His left. Roods commonly stood at the east end of a cathedral NAVE and were finally removed during the first years of the reign of Elizabeth I. They were generally placed on a ROOD BEAM over the ROOD SCREEN.

ROOD BEAM the beam at the entrance of a church chancel that supports a large cross or crucifix (ROOD).

ROOD SCREEN in cathedrals such screens are generally referred to as CHOIR SCREENS.

ROSE WINDOW a circular window with tracery radiating from the centre.

SECULAR CATHEDRAL a medieval English cathedral under the jurisdiction of the DEAN and CHAPTER rather than of monks. After the Reformation these cathedrals were known as of the 'Old Foundation' while the former monastic cathedrals were given new constitutions. These, and the new Henrician bishoprics (for example, Gloucester, Bristol, Oxford, Peterborough and Chester) are cathedrals of the 'New Foundation'.

SEDILIA canopied stone seats provided for the clergy on the south side of the high altar.

SEE an alternative word for an episcopal DIOCESE deriving from the Latin *sedes* or 'seat' (the bishop's CATHEDRA).

SHRINE the venerated tomb of a saint containing relics in a FERETORY. From the Latin *scrinium* ('a chest').

SPIRE a tall pyramidal or conical structure crowning a cathedral tower. Spires were commonly of wood and covered in lead (as at Durham and Lincoln), though certain major examples such as Salisbury, Norwich and Chichester are of stone.

STALL a fixed seat for the officiating clergy in the CHOIR of a cathedral.

TIERCONS extra decorative ribs springing from the corners of a bay.

TRACERY the openwork pattern of masonry in a Gothic window.

TRANSEPT the arms of a cruciform church to the north and south of the crossing.

TRANSLATION the transference of the relics of a saint from one location to another. Often marked by a separate feast day (as in the cases of St Thomas à Becket and St Ethedreda).

TRIFORIM the middle storey of a Gothic church treated as an arcaded wall passage.

UNDERCROFT the vaulted crypt generally situated under the eastern parts of a CATHEDRAL (as at Rochester and Canterbury).

BIBLIOGRAPHY

Britton's Cathedrals

Britton, J., *The History and Antiquities of the See and Cathedral Church of Salisbury* (Longman, Hurst, Rees, Orme and Brown, 1814)

Britton, J., *The History and Antiquities of the See and Cathedral Church of Norwich* (Longman, Hurst, Rees, Orme and Brown, 1816)

Britton, J., *The History and Antiquities of the See and Cathedral Church of Winchester* (Longman, Hurst, Rees, Orme and Brown, 1817)

Britton, J., *The History and Antiquities of the Metropolitical Church of York* (Longman, Hurst, Rees, Orme and Brown, 1819)

Britton, J., *The History and Antiquities of the See and Cathedral Church of Lichfield* (Longman, Hurst, Rees, Orme and Brown, 1820)

Britton, J., *The History and Antiquities of the Metropolitical Church of Canterbury* (Longman, Hurst, Rees, Orme and Brown, 1821)

Britton, J., *The History and Antiquities of the Cathedral Church of Oxford* (Longman, Hurst, Rees, Orme and Brown, 1821)

Britton, J., *The History and Antiquities of the Cathedral Church of Wells* (Longman, Hurst, Rees, Orme and Brown, 1824)

Britton, J., *The History and Antiquities of the Cathedral Church of Exeter* (Longman, Rees, Orme, Brown and Green, 1826)

Britton, J., *The History and Antiquities of the Abbey and Cathedral Church of Peterborough* (Longman, Rees, Orme, Brown and Green, 1828)

Britton, J., *The History and Antiquities of the Abbey and Cathedral Church of Gloucester* (Longman, Rees, Orme, Brown and Green, 1829)

Britton, J., *The History and Antiquities of the Abbey and Cathedral Church of Bristol* (Longman, Rees, Orme, Brown and Green, 1830)

Britton, J., *The History and Antiquities of the Cathedral Church of Hereford* (Longman, Rees, Orme, Brown and Green, 1831)

Britton, J., *The History and Antiquities of the Cathedral Church of Worcester* (Longman, Rees, Orme, Brown, Green and T. Longman, 1835)

Murray's Handbooks

King, R.J., *Handbook to the Northern Cathedrals*, 2 vols (John Murray, 1869)

King, R.J., *Handbook to the Southern Cathedrals*, 2 vols (John Murray, 1876)

King, R.J., *Handbook to the Western Cathedrals* (John Murray, 1874)

Milman, H.H., *Handbook to Saint Paul's Cathedral* (John Murray, 1879)

Venables, E., *Handbook to the Eastern Cathedrals* (John Murray, 1880)

Bell's Cathedral Series

Addleshaw, P., *The Cathedral Church of Exeter* (George Bell & Sons, 1899)

Bygate, J.E., *The Cathedral Church of Durham* (George Bell & Sons, 1899)

Clifton, A.B., *The Cathedral Church of Lichfield* (George Bell & Sons, 1899)

Clutton Brock, A., *The Cathedral Church of York* (George Bell & Sons, 1907)

Corlette, H.C., *The Cathedral Church of Chichester* (George Bell & Sons, 1901)

Dearmer, Revd P., *The Cathedral Church of Oxford* (George Bell & Sons, 1899)

Dearmer, Revd P., *The Cathedral Church of Wells* (George Bell & Sons, 1899)

Dimock, Revd A., *The Cathedral Church of Saint Paul* (George Bell & Sons, 1900)

Fisher, A.H., *The Cathedral Church of Hereford* (George Bell & Sons, 1899)

Hiatt, C., *The Cathedral Church of Chester* (George Bell & Sons, 1899)

Kendrick, A.F., *The Cathedral Church of Lincoln* (George Bell & Sons, 1898)

Massé, H.J.L.J., *The Cathedral Church of Gloucester* (George Bell & Sons, 1899)

Massé, H.J.L.J., *The Cathedral Church of Bristol* (George Bell & Sons, 1901)

Palmer, G.H., *The Cathedral Church of Rochester* (George Bell & Sons, 1907)

Perkins, Revd T., *An Itinerary of the English Cathedrals for the Use of Travellers* (George Bell & Sons, 1905)

Quennell, C.H.B., *The Cathedral Church of Norwich* (George Bell & Sons, 1907)

Sergeant, P.W. *The Cathedral Church of Winchester* (George Bell & Sons, 1898)

Strange, E.F., *The Cathedral Church of Worcester* (George Bell & Sons, 1908)

Sweeting, Revd W.D., *The Cathedral Church of Peterborough* (George Bell & Sons, 1898)

Sweeting, Revd W.D., *The Cathedral Church of Ely* (George Bell & Sons, 1901)

White, G., *The Cathedral Church of Salisbury* (George Bell & Sons, 1898)

Withers, H., *The Cathedral Church of Canterbury* (George Bell & Sons, 1897)

Studies of Churches, Styles and Architects

Amery, C., Richardson, M. and Stamp, G., *Lutyens* (Arts Council of Great Britain, 1982)

Austin, R.W.J. (ed. & trans.), *The Rites of Durham* (Dean & Chapter of Durham, 1985)

Briggs, M.S., *Goths and Vandals: A Study of the Destruction, Neglect and Preservation of Historical Buildings in England* (Constable, 1952)

Brogan, Revd B., *The Great Link: A History of St George's Southwark* (Burns Oates, 1948)

Cobb, G., *English Cathedrals: The Forgotten Centuries* (Thames & Hudson, 1980)

Coldstream, N., *The Decorated Style* (British Museum Press, 1994)

Cole, D., *The Work of Sir Gilbert Scott* (The Architectural Press, 1980)

De l'Hôpital, W., *Westminster Cathedral and its Architect* (Hutchinson, 1919)

Downes, K., *Christopher Wren* (Allen Lane, Penguin, 1971)

Downes, K. (ed.), *Sir Christopher Wren and the Making of St Paul's* (Royal Academy of Arts, 1991)

Ferrey, B., *Recollections of A.W.N. Pugin* (Edward Stamford, 1861)

Ferriday, P., *Lord Grimthorpe 1816–1905* (John Murray, 1957)

Foster, A., *Pevsner Architectural Guides: Birmingham* (Yale University Press, 2005)

Foyle, A., *Pevsner Architectural Guides: Bristol* (Yale University Press, 2004)

Gwynn, D., *Lord Shrewsbury, Pugin and the Gothic Revival* (Hollis & Carter, 1946)

Hartwell, C., *Pevsner Architectural Guides: Manchester* (Yale University Press, 2002)

Harvey, J., *Henry Yevele* (BT Batsford,1946)

Harvey, J., *English Cathedrals* (BT Batsford, 1956)

Harvey, J., *The Perpendicular Style* (BT Batsford, 1978)

Harwood, E., *Pevsner Architectural Guides: Nottingham* (Yale University Press, 2008)

Herbert, A., Martin, P. and Thomas, G. (eds.), *St Albans: Cathedral & Abbey* (Scala Publishers, 2002)

Higham, F., *Southwark Story* (Hodder & Stoughton, 1955)

Hope, V. & Lloyd, J., *Exeter Cathedral: A Short History & Description* (Exeter, 1973)

Hussey, C., *The Life of Sir Edwin Lutyens* (Country Life, 1950)

Keene, D., Burns, A. & Saint, A. (eds.), *St. Paul's: The Cathedral Church of London 604–2004* (Yale University Press, 2004)

Kennerley, P., *The Building of Liverpool Cathedral* (Carnegie Publishing, 1991)

Martin, C., *A Glimpse of Heaven: Catholic Churches in England and Wales* (English Heritage, 2006)

McCombie, G., *Pevsner Architectural Guides: Newcastle and Gateshead* (Yale University Press, 2009)

Nairn, I. & Pevsner, N., *The Buildings of England: Sussex* (Penguin Books, 1965)

O'Donnell, R., *The Pugins and the Catholic Midlands* (Archdiocese of Birmingham, 2002)

Orme, N., *Exeter Cathedral as it Was 1050–1550* (Devon Books, 1986)

Quiney, A., *John Loughborough Pearson* (Yale University Press, 1979)

Robert, M., *Durham* (BT Batsford/English Heritage, 1994)

Robinson, J.M., *James Wyatt: Architect to George III* (Yale University Press, 2012)

Rogers, P., *Westminster Cathedral: An Illustrated History* (Oremus, 2012)

Runcie, R. (ed.), *Cathedral and City: St Albans Ancient and Modern* (Martyn Associates, 1977)

Scott, G.G., *Personal and Professional Recollections* (Sampson Low, 1879)

Sharples, J., *Pevsner Architectural Guides: Liverpool* (Yale University Press 2004)

Stanton, P., *Pugin* (Thames & Hudson, 1971)

Stevens, Revd, T.P., *The Story of Southwark Cathedral* (Marston & Co 1922)

Symondson, A., *Stephen Dykes Bower* (RIBA Publishing, 2011)

Tatton-Brown, T., *The English Cathedral* (New Holland, 2002)

Taylor, N., *Looking at Cathedrals* (BBC Publications, 1968)

Vale, E., *Junior Heritage Books: Cathedrals* (BT Batsford, 1957)

Verey, D. & Welander, D., *Gloucester Cathedral* (Alan Sutton, 1989)

Whinney, M., *Wren*, (Thames & Hudson, 1971)

Wilson, C., *The Gothic Cathedral* (Thames & Hudson, 1990)

Wrathmell, S., *Pevsner Architectural Guides: Leeds* (Yale University Press 2005)

PICTURE CREDITS

INDEX